HOW TO PLAY THE PIANO

MARK HAMBOURG

HOW TO
PLAY THE PIANO

BY

MARK HAMBOURG

WITH PRACTICAL ILLUSTRATIONS AND
DIAGRAMS AND AN ABRIDGED COMPEN-
DIUM OF FIVE-FINGER EXERCISES, SCALES,
THIRDS, ARPEGGI, OCTAVES **AS**
PRACTISED BY HIM

THEODORE PRESSER CO.
1712 CHESTNUT STREET
•PHILADELPHIA•

DEDICATED TO MY FRIEND
D. MUIR

FOREWORD

MARK HAMBOURG was born in Bogutchar in the province of Voronesh, South Russia, on May 30th, 1879, and showed promise of great musical talent at such an early age that his father, himself a professor of advanced piano-playing, personally took his musical education in hand, and brought him out at Moscow as a juvenile prodigy in 1889, afterwards taking him to tour in England. In 1891 he left London, whither his family had migrated, and went to study under Leschctitzky in Vienna, where he remained three years. After winning the Liszt Scholarship during that period, he made his debut as a full-grown pianist in 1894 at a Philharmonic Concert in Vienna under the conductorship of Dr. Richter, and a year later made his bow to the London public at a concert of the Philharmonic Society, following this up by giving four recitals of his own as well as fulfilling a number of important engagements in the principal cities of Europe.

In 1895 came Mark Hambourg's first Australian tour, which was a sensational success. During the following year he played at many important concerts in England before leaving for a second tour in Australia in 1897. For two years after the conclusion of this tour Mark Hambourg devoted himself more particularly to general study, his public activity being confined to a few concerts in England, Germany and Switzerland. This period of study paved the way for further achievements during the first American tour upon which he embarked in the autumn of 1899. A period of great activity followed in England and on the Continent, the pianist's engagements including a series of recitals at the Queen's Hall, appearances at the Cardiff Festival in 1902, and at Lamoureux and Colonne Concerts in Paris.

A second American tour of 80 concerts, followed by a third visit to Australia and a tour in South Africa, which latter was undertaken primarily for change and rest, but which proved also to be a most successful venture, fully occupied Mark Hambourg's time until 1906, especially as he had to fulfil many engagements in England as well. His recital at the Queen's Hall on June 18th of the same year marked his one thousandth appearance in public. In 1907 he made his second tour in South Africa, which occupied the whole of that spring and summer. In October of the same year followed a third American tour, while in July, 1908, after a great farewell concert at the Albert Hall, which was attended by over 6000 people, came a fourth visit to Australia extending over six months.

He has been twice touring all over Canada and then again throughout Europe. In 1914 he was in the United States for the fourth time. Mark Hambourg's activities are ever on the increase, and during the year 1920 he played over 120 recitals in Great Britain alone, while since he has been continuously playing in Paris, on the Continent generally, and all over the world.

CONTENTS

PART ONE: HOW TO PLAY THE PIANO

PART TWO: ABRIDGED COMPENDIUM OF EXERCISES, ETC., FOR THE USE OF STUDENTS

The fingering used in this book is the Continental fingering.

PART ONE

HOW TO PLAY THE PIANO

HOW TO PLAY THE PIANO

CHAPTER I

PROLOGUE: PREPARING FOR THE PIANIST'S CAREER

LET us consider a little what possibilities and difficulties await the youth who desires nowadays to take up the piano professionally, and carve out a career for himself with its aid. It is, first of all, necessary to bear in mind that the present-day public demands greater attainment than ever before from executant artists. At least the case is rather that the existing conditions under which we live tend to make all endeavour very strenuous, therefore it grows increasingly hard to arrive at distinction in any walk of life.

COMPETITION IN THE MUSICAL WORLD

To begin with, competition is very great, and in the musical world there are many more artists, and many more concerts than formerly; also though the best talent is still most rare and precious, yet the general level of achievement is no doubt a good deal higher than it used to be. The young student therefore must seriously consider the outlook in front of him before he decides to take up the arduous career of a pianist, and I need scarcely mention that his first business should be to try and ascertain whether he has a decided disposition for the instrument. Unless he possesses this, it is in the highest degree a waste of time for him to commence the study of it at all.

Of course it is hard for the young, or even for friends around them to determine the exact measure of their capacity at the outset, for real talent is in itself a fusion of so many different qualities. The gift or inborn disposition for music does not necessarily develop into true talent in the sense in which I understand it, namely, as a certain power containing within it elements which are able to bring forth great superiority of attainment in whatsoever branch of the human intelligence they actuate. It is strange that

13

the faculty of easy musical expression alone is not enough to ensure success, though people have often been deluded into thinking so, and thereby much bitter disappointment and misery have been caused to unrecognized aspirants after fame.

How many there are who give the impression of being astonishingly endowed with the musical instinct, and even possess what is known as perfect pitch, which appears to be an unerring discrimination of the ear between the various sounds of the scale. Such people certainly seem to have a wonderful natural facility in all things appertaining to music, yet they often do not arrive at any particular eminence in the profession.   One is told that it is such a pity "So and So" has such a genius for music, but is so lazy he will not work, or so nervous he cannot do himself justice, or that some other drawback hinders him!   But the fact probably is, in cases like these, that the musical propensity is there no doubt, sometimes even in a high measure, but the necessary talent or power is not present with it, to enable it to attain a successful development.

What, then, should the student seek for in himself when he feels that he has the gift of music and wonders whether he possesses sufficient talent accompanying it to succeed professionally?   Well, he must consider, amongst other things, if he is capable of many years of hard unremitting work at the development of the technical side of his art.   He must also find in himself physical endurance, courage, coolness in emergency, command of nerves, determination, inexhaustible patience, self-confidence, and, above all, such a love of his art for its own sake as will carry him over every disappointment.

THE BEST TEACHER

But allowing that he has the signs within him of all these needful qualities, or at least he thinks he has, and he decides to take up the study of the piano seriously, he has then to make up his mind about his first practical necessity, and this is undoubtedly to go and learn with the very best teacher he can procure.   There is nothing that helps so much as to be really well taught from the very beginning.   So many artists have had to go through irksome and irritating labour in later life, and lost much valuable time in having to undo the effects of bad tuition in student days.   It is therefore an enormous benefit to the beginner if whoever is responsible for his education insists on his being sent from the outset to a really good and experienced professor.   At this early stage, also, I estimate it as most important that the student, though he should work regularly and conscientiously, should not study for too long at a time.

Personally I have always found that two hours at a stretch of careful practice is quite enough at one sitting, and it is far better to do several periods of work in the day of shorter duration than to be at it for many hours together. The mind and ear only become confused after a protracted time of work by the constant blur of sound and then the practising degenerates into merely senseless repetitions without discrimination. Besides which the fatigue and strain put upon the nerves by such protracted study are very injurious to the young student's health, and tend to impair his constitution before any of the wear and tear of his profession begin.

TAKE CARE OF THE STUDENT'S HEALTH

Here let me say, that it is most important to remember to look after the physical health of the youthful pianist, and to build up his strength by constant exercise and fresh air, for later on if he is to be successful, he will have to be fit to endure every sort of strain, such as long hours in the train, much nervous excitement, great bodily fatigue. I am perfectly certain that good health and strength are absolutely indispensable to the modern professional pianist, and the sort of notion that an artist consists generally of a pale and sickly creature with delicate lungs and over-strung nerves is a conception of fiction! High strung, his profession will make him, and sensitive, but he must have his nerves well under control and healthy, otherwise he will never survive the tension of public life.

There is no doubt that the unaccountable failures of some people with really great talents, who deserved recognition, have been due to their neglect of health and their consequent inability through sheer physical weakness to face the tests put upon them. Just think what a long concert tour means to the artist in the way of endurance! Night after night appearing in big important engagements, with all the responsibility they entail; day after day long journeys by train or steamer, often many nights travelling too; yet, in spite of all that, on arrival he must always be ready to play with energy, spirit and unflagging interest, otherwise he will not inspire or convince his audience. The faculty of interesting and carrying away his hearers by the power of his imagination working upon them through the music, is another quality most needful to the artist. If he is to succeed he must acquire it, or rather develop it, and it can only come through his learning to sink himself in whatsoever he is playing to such a degree that his whole soul and mind become one with the music he is interpreting, and thus it speaks forth with mesmeric conviction to the listeners around him.

I suppose one could fill volumes if one wished to descant upon all the points which go to the making of a fine pianist. But this is only meant to be a general introduction to my remarks on the study of the piano, which I have been asked to write for students and others who may be interested in the subject. I can therefore only touch here, as they occur to me, upon a few of the most salient essentials for those who intend to go in for the profession.

DEVELOPING THE MUSICAL MEMORY

Having spoken of good tuition, hard work and health, I come to another vital consideration, namely, the development of a reliable memory. It has become the fashion for all instrumental soloists to perform in public by heart; it is a habit that has only grown up in the last thirty years, and I do not know that it is always a good one. For the mere presence of the music upon the piano will often give greater confidence to the nervous performer, and ensure his giving a good account of his work, while the absence of it may so obsess his mind with the fear of forgetting that he will be unable to let himself go in the interpretation which he had prepared. However, the public generally, more or less, expects that the pianist should play from memory, and probably, if he has no fear of its failing him, he does under these circumstances give a freer and consequently more inspired rendering of his music. At any rate, it is an urgent point to cultivate a good memory.

With many musicians this memory is a gift of itself, and needs only constant and ordered use to make it perfectly reliable. On the other hand, there are frequent instances of very great artists whose memory will play them tricks, and from one cause or another even the best of them have been known to fail at times, often merely from over-fatigue, ill-health, or some preoccupation. One of the most extraordinary examples of this happened to a very famous pianist at a concert. He was playing the Concerto of Beethoven in C minor and had arrived at the second subject of the beautiful slow movement which starts with a very similar progression to the beginning of the second subject in the Adagio of Mendelssohn's Concerto in G minor. The pianist started the Beethoven second subject correctly, and then in a moment of oblivion wandered away into the one in the Mendelssohn Concerto to the astonishment of the audience and his own dismay when he realized what he was doing! It is said that this particular artist never would play in public again without his music, so greatly had he been upset by the occurrence.

The pianist has also to learn to control himself in the emergency of forgetting, which is one of the most agonizing experiences that an artist can undergo in public. But if he can only keep his presence of mind, he can often extricate himself from his predicament with the aid of his musical instinct, and that sometimes so cleverly, that his lapse will pass unnoticed by any save the most knowing amongst the audience. To do this of course needs great command of nerve on the part of the performer, but as in every public career emergencies do arise occasionally, it is an essential part of the professional artist's equipment that he should know how to meet them.

His own nervousness is one of the worst demons he has to combat. Even very experienced players suffer from this on the concert platform; in fact, as the artist gets older and understands his responsibilities better he will feel, as a rule, more nervous than the youth who does not realize so much. But his greater experience will help him naturally to obtain the mastery over this difficulty, and even to turn the inner excitement it causes to good account. For when he can command it, this tension of the nerves will stimulate the brain to greater activity and thus will help the performer to give a more vivid interpretation to the music than if he was feeling quite cold and indifferent. I have never known any really fine artist who did not sometimes suffer from nervousness in public, but that need not frighten the beginner, as through constant playing in concerts he will acquire the habit of the platform to a certain extent, and gain the necessary control over himself.

MINOR DIFFICULTIES

Many minor upsets in the way of small emergencies may occur at any time during a concert which also the artist must not allow to put him out. For instance, he may have a difficult or unsympathetic conductor, if it is an orchestral concert, or the orchestra may be poor and unreliable, and come in at the wrong places. It once happened to me that the wrong parts had been brought for the orchestra, and when I came in to play and sat down, prepared with the E Flat Concerto of Liszt, to my horror they gaily started the opening bars of the Saint-Saëns' Concerto in C minor! There was no time to protest, the audience was sitting expectant. Luckily I knew the other concerto and so followed bravely on with it, but I was certainly not prepared to play it at a moment's notice in public, without looking through it first!

That contretemps arose from having no time to rehearse, and I earnestly counsel all young pianists to insist upon a rehearsal when playing with the orchestra wherever possible, no matter how much extra travelling or fatigue it may cause them. For it is almost out of the question to obtain a really satisfactory performance of a work from anyone's standpoint by just scrambling through it, in terror all the time lest the orchestra should not follow you, as happens when concertos are played in public without rehearsal. Of course if the artist has done the same concerto many times with the same conductor and orchestra, and they well know the rendering he gives of the work, the case is rather different. Under such conditions the pianist would be justified, if there was any difficulty about a rehearsal, in doing without one, but even then it is far better for the young artist to make a point of it.

There are two other things I would like to speak about before closing this chapter, which are in close connection with the pianist's outlook upon life. The first is, that I do recommend him most sincerely not to neglect his general education and risk becoming what used to be called " music simple! " Music is such an absorbing study, and taken professionally it uses up so much energy and mind power, that it is difficult I know sometimes to keep up interest in many other subjects at the same time, especially during student years. But I am certain that it is an inestimable advantage to the virtuoso to have his brain alive to every branch of intellectual endeavour. For the broader and more enlightened his vision of life, so much the finer and profounder his own art will become.

NEVER PLAY DOWN TO AN AUDIENCE

Secondly, though not quite in the category of what I have just been saying, yet relative to the same high conception of his art, I greatly urge the young professional never to play down to an audience. By this I mean, never to be persuaded to play second-rate music to a certain class of public on the plea that they are not sufficiently educated to appreciate the best. This is the greatest possible fallacy, as I know by experience, for I have played all over the world to every sort and condition and class of people, and I have always found that they respect and are interested in one's art even when they do not quite understand it all, and that they appreciate and desire the best a man can do. The artist should always try to stimulate his public up to the highest kind of music and never sink to clap-trap in order to entice their passing fancy. Otherwise, though they may enjoy themselves for the moment, they will not want to come again and he will be lowered in their estimation to the level of what they have heard from him.

To play up to the highest standard ought to be the cardinal maxim of the young pianist, and then with hard work, enthusiasm and unfailing resolution he will in time make his way up the steep ladder into first rank and win the rewards of success.

Chapter II

HOW TO PRACTISE

I AM devoting this chapter entirely to the subject of how to practise the piano, and shall try to point out here what I have found from my experience to be the most efficacious way of setting about it.

Broadly speaking, the cardinal rules to be observed in all practising should be, first, great attention to detail; second, avoidance of over-fatigue, both mental and physical. It is also most necessary for the attainment of the best results to set up from the outset some fixed schedule of practising. Systematically ordered work is such an inestimable help in all stages of piano-playing, but more especially in the elementary one, as I myself well know, for I had the good fortune to start my pianoforte education with teachers who were steeped in the best traditions. My first one was my father, Prof. Michael Hambourg, who had been a pupil of Nicholas Rubinstein; while my second, the famous Leschetitzky, had studied with Czerny.

And Czerny especially represents the school of pianoforte playing which has produced many of the greatest pianists of modern times, his influence extending through Liszt, Anton Rubinstein, Tausig, etc., down to many famous pianists of to-day. Therefore I am a great believer in starting to study according to a good method, or school, as we call it. Such a method will train the mind and fingers in a definite and organized trend of technical development.

Of course, it is a good thing as well to acquire a theoretical and general musical education, but I think, especially in the training of children who intend to become professionals later on, that it is imperative that their main energy and time should be directed first of all to learning how to master the technical difficulties of their instrument. I do not believe that musical children learn much away from the piano, at least they cannot acquire the actual mechanical facility of playing except at the keyboard. I wish to lay stress on this fact, because there are in fashion just now so many clever ways of educating children musically. For instance, they are taught how to compose fugues in imitation of Bach after a few hours of tuition, etc. This kind of instruction is doubtless of advantage in stimulating general musical knowledge and, above all, for training unmusical little ones and developing the faculty which might otherwise be completely lost to them, but in the education of the young pianist such systems must never be allowed to obscure the main issue, which has always to be, first of all, the acquirement of absolute proficiency at the keyboard.

Practice in early childhood should never be for a period of more than half an hour, and the whole amount to be done should not exceed one hour. Also care ought to be taken to procure music for children to study which will appeal to their imaginations, and even their exercises should be in pleasant forms of sound, which will help to keep them interested. And the best thing is to instil as soon as possible into the mind of the child the desire for beauty of touch and clearness of execution.

NO CHILD SHOULD PRACTISE ALONE

No child ought to be left to practise by himself; someone should always sit with him and see that he gives each note its full value. To attain this object it is excellent to make the little one count out aloud while playing. The pedal should never be permitted, and each hand ought to be practised separately. For if the two hands are worked together the concentration of the mind is divided, instead of being directed to one thing at a time. Besides, a certain amount of covering up of the sound goes on when both hands are playing, which is bad, and impedes clearness of execution and conception of the difficulties to be contended with.

These remarks about the separate practice of each hand are intended to apply mainly to the purely mechanical exercises, such as are used for the articulation of the fingers, etc. It is important, also, that such exercises should be easy and not strain the hand, for very serious results can develop from overstraining of the hand in childhood. Exercises and scales must be practised in all the keys, not only in C major in which they are generally written, as it is of great benefit to the child to be able to play as easily in one key as another. Another good maxim to be observed is not to allow exercises to be repeated *ad nauseam*, over and over again, as the mind only gets bewildered with the unceasing repetitions, and no result can then be obtained.

I am speaking here at some length about the practising of a child, as, if the routine of good systematic work is acquired in early youth, it becomes a habit and continues naturally throughout life.

I now arrive at a further stage, when, having been carefully initiated, the young student begins to consider the piano as his life-work. His problem then becomes that of all pianists, both great and small, namely and principally, how to practise in such a way as to obtain the maximum of economy in time and effort, to keep always fresh in mind and to avoid too much repetition.

Generally I advise that the average practice of an advanced student and, indeed, of any pianist, be not more than five hours a day, and not less than three, under ordinary circumstances. Those who have no technical talent at all and have great difficulty in acquiring adequate mastery of means, or those whose musical memory is weak, can practise more, and often do, but on the whole very extended hours of study only tend to staleness. In any case the student should devise a systematic way of dividing up his hours of practice if he wants to get the best profit out of his work. For until he has experience in concert playing and the frequent opportunity of performing in public (which thing, of course, impedes practising and also obviates to some extent the necessity of it), he must always give a certain definite time every day to purely technical study.

A REGULAR DAILY COURSE

To this end the pianist ought to draw up for himself a regular course to be pursued, such as the following. First, a short space should always be given to finger technique, ten minutes of scales, ten minutes of arpeggi. Scales to be played in four different keys each day, with their accompanying arpeggi in every development, also the chromatic and contrary motion scales. Thus if four scales in four different keys are done each day, the whole range of scales will be got through every three days. After these scales ten or twelve *five-finger* exercises, comprising all the positions of the hand, can be worked at. Hanon's and Czerny's Exercises are the ones which I particularly recommend; they are quite excellent for helping to acquire an even and rapid articulation of the fingers. Also as the student advances he should add Moszkowski's school of thirds and sixths to his daily round.

The reason why all this technical daily study is so essential is, because to obtain a supple, easy mastery of the piano, it is necessary to possess a real athletic agility of fingers, hands and arms. And just as an athlete in training does a fixed amount of regular exercises every day, to keep the muscles of his whole body in elasticity and fitness, so must the pianist go through a similar process to train his arms, hands and fingers.

COMMON SENSE PRACTICE

Now there are many common sense axioms to be observed in the details of practising, which the student will find out by experience. For instance, if he has to play on a certain day a piece in which many octaves and double notes occur, he should on that day make a point of practising only scales and exercises for the simple articulation of the fingers. He should take care during his working hours not to study the same octave and double-note techniques as are to be found in the piece that he will be playing later on in the day, for if he does so he will risk suffering from lameness of the hands. Such lameness will appear from working the hands too long in certain extended positions as are peculiar to octave playing, etc. Therefore great variety of motion must always be aimed at, in order to keep the hands fresh and vigorous. Also should the student experience the slightest fatigue in the hand when playing scales and passages, let him instantly cease until that feeling has quite passed away.

OCTAVE EXERCISES

Much practising of octave exercises should ever be avoided, for as the action used in playing octaves is a good deal produced by the contraction of the muscles of the forearm, continuous work of this sort tends to strain them, and generates a sort of cramp which is very difficult to cure. Personally, I think that students should only study octaves when absolutely imperative for some piece they are learning, and then, if they used Kullak's Octave Exercises, they will find them amongst the very best of their kind.

If I had to pronounce an opinion as to what I had found to be the most absolute essential of a physical kind for a pianist's equipment, I think I should declare for a perfectly supple and loose wrist. How few students consider this acquirement enough, yet it is the secret of all softness and roundness of attack, all brilliancy and finish of passage playing, all grace of expression. He who forces the tone and gets harsh, unpleasant sounds from his instrument—the unfortunate, who, after many hours of hard work finds himself hopelessly incapacitated by a sudden swelling in one of the tendons of his arm, or a stiffness in his hand—both these are always victims of want of care given to the development of a supple wrist. Without perfect freedom of action, there is no real power or elasticity, no proper play for the fingers, and the performer will generally fail at the critical moment in difficult rapid passages.

There are many schools of piano playing, various of which advocate lifting the fingers as high as possible off the keyboard, with a view to acquiring greater power, but I cannot help thinking that the tone thus produced is of a hard, disagreeable nature, and the time lost by such high articulation detrimental to the smoothness and rapidity which are so necessary. Myself, I greatly advocate keeping the fingers close to the instrument and pressing the keys, thus giving the sound a warmer and more elastic quality and modifying the naturally more or less wooden tone which pianists have always to contend against to a certain extent even in the finest pianos, by reason of their constitution, as compared with stringed instruments.

I do not find elaborate studies very efficacious for the purely mechanical development of technique, as the embellishments and harmonies which make the palatableness of such studies only distract the student's mind away from the main point of advancing the technical power, and thus cause loss of time and effort. For the only really valuable study is that which concentrates its whole energy in pursuing the true object to be achieved in each particular branch of work. And it is far more profitable to practise for a short time with absolute concentration on the technical problem in order definitely to surmount it, than to pass several more or less wasteful hours dallying with the difficulties wrapped up as they are in elaborate studies with a pleasant gilding of harmonies and progressions.

Also, many of the studies which are given to students with a view to helping them technically are in themselves bad music as well as indifferent mechanical aids. Of course, these remarks with regard to studies in general are certainly not meant to include real concert studies, such as those of Chopin, Liszt, etc., but it is scarcely necessary to say that these are not purely studies for technique, but are rather beautiful musical problems to be unravelled when a certain amount of facility has already been acquired by the student.

Advanced students should also endeavour in their practising to prepare themselves along certain lines of study, with a view to making a repertoire of pieces, which will be useful to them when the time comes for them to make up programmes for their concerts.

Now as regards how to start the study of a piece, it is as well first of all to look at it from the technical point of view alone. For until means have been mastered no proper musical expression or interpretation can be adequately conveyed. First of all, then, the pianist ought to dissect the piece from the mechanical side and find out where the most difficult passages occur. Technically speaking, of course, all pieces are merely collections of scales, thirds, passages, etc., harmonically treated in different ways and used as the vehicles to express the composer's ideas.

MASTERING DIFFICULT PASSAGES

Having decided which are the most awkward passages to master in his piece, the student should not then just play them over and over again, as so many do, hoping that by much repetition the difficulties will finally be surmounted. He must rather play his passages once or twice, then stop and think about them for a minute, and try to get a clear definition of them in his mind. Then start afresh, and having worked a little more, pause again. By thus stopping to think and keep his mind lucid he will both master and retain passages with much greater ease and rapidity than by confusing his mind through continuous reiteration without ever pausing to listen properly or to consider what the passage should sound like.

It is also a very good thing when first learning a piece to divide it, taking, say, each eight bars or so at a time to work at, and thus getting to know the component parts well before reviewing the work as a whole. Another branch of practising which is too aften neglected by the young pianist is the study of the bass or frame work of the music he learns. Many times one hears something played in such a way that the bass part is completely swallowed up, and nothing can be heard but the right hand. This defect is the more difficult to conquer, because the left hand, to which the bass in entrusted, is naturally with most people the feebler member. Yet weakness in the bass parts is a very serious fault, for it often undermines the whole construction of a piece and upsets all the harmonies. After all, music, like everything else, must have a good, stable foundation. Therefore the student must give much care and attention to the bass parts of his piece.

I cannot end this chapter about practising better than by earnestly recommending all students, from the very outset, to apply themselves to the diligent study of the works of Bach. There is no composer whose music is so well calculated to give the best and most detailed knowledge of polyphonic playing in addition to perfect freedom of technique in both hands and independence of action and thought. It also goes without saying that constant work among Bach's masterpieces of intellect and feeling are of immeasurable value in developing the whole artistic taste and understanding of the mind.

Chapter III

ON TECHNIQUE GENERALLY

The bare word technique, when applied to pianoforte playing, seems often to give people an erroneous impression of its real significance. It seems to mean to them just the power of being able to play very rapidly, and also to perform very difficult passages, upon the keyboard, and often the word seems to carry with it a strange sort of odium to certain kinds of music-lovers. "A wonderful technician," they cry, about some pianist, "but nothing more."

How can this prejudice against great development of technique have arisen? I think that it is just because technique is sometimes considered as meaning only that one-sided capability of being able to move the fingers and hands with special agility—"digital dexterity," as the critics call it!

That particular capacity is no doubt a very important and necessary branch of technique on the piano, but it is only one small part of the whole immense subject; and the pianist who has given all his attention to that branch alone can certainly not be called in the best sense of the word a great technician, nor can he arrive at the highest results with only that development.

SIGNIFIES PERFECT ATTAINMENT

Technique in pianoforte playing, as in all other arts, signifies far more than agility and rapidity of finger action. Rather does its perfect attainment comprise within itself every means of expression that it is possible for the artist pianist to command. Thus technique represents to him in all its varying branches, endurance, tone or colour production, touch, intensity of feeling, phrasing, elegance of execution, symmetry of detail. And the man who has only studied and can merely produce agility, has but acquired one-fifth part of pianoforte technique; therefore how can he be the highest kind of artist, if, indeed, a real artist at all!

Now I believe that many people have the imagination and the emotions of the artistic temperament, but these qualities with them lack outlet for want of adequate means of expression. They cannot give a vent to their thoughts, because they do not possess the technical development sufficient to enable them to do so. Technique should therefore comprise the mastery of all means of self-expression in music, and on the piano especially can no player afford to neglect any manual facility that tends in the long run to help him arrive at the summit of interpretation. For it stands to reason that the more physical capacity the artist possesses for clothing his thoughts, the less hampered will he be in giving expression to the best that is in him.

AN INFALLIBLE TEST

The artists who have really great command of means are the ones who, no matter how hard or elaborate in musical writing the passages are which they have to play, manage to make those passages sound so beautiful and full of expression that the listener will never notice whether the music that is being performed is difficult or not, so absorbed will he be in the delight the playing gives him. How much consummate technique is there sometimes expended upon the execution of a quite simple melody, slow, soft and melting, the tones flowing into each other, so that no one who listens can realize that the piano which is being played is only a mechanical instrument with hammers that strike upon copper strings. What patience and study, too, is needed to develop the deep sonority of touch in massive chords, and the light brilliancy of rippling progressions.

All this is impossible without technical command, and it is only when mastery of every kind of vehicle for expression has been acquired that interpretation can be approached with confidence. There is no greater suffering to the artist than to have in his mind a certain impression which the music has created in it, and not to be able to reproduce the picture on his piano, because he has shortcomings in technique which deter him. On the other hand, what joy it is to a pianist to resume the playing of some great masterpiece, which he had studied diligently in former years, and at that time had never succeeded in giving to it the rendering that he sought, owing to insufficient mastery of means. But upon starting upon it again after this long period during which he had doubtless been developing gradually, and probably unconsciously, he finds that now he can at last do with ease what he wants in the piece, and which he never could arrive at before. To attain such a reward is worth all the labours of Hercules!

A GREAT FALLACY

It is a great fallacy to think that it is more difficult to play passages and intricate ornamentation in music very fast, or very loud, than softly and at a moderate speed. It is often the contrary which is the case. Pianists sometimes increase their tone and their *tempo* more than they intend to do through nervousness and want of confidence or from fear of failure of memory. The pianist who can play a long series of intricate and more or less rapid successions of passages in a slow *tempo*, and *pianissimo*, with a lot of rhythm, is often doing thereby something that is actually harder to achieve than the more showy splash-dash which to the uninitiated might seem most wonderful.

Of course the greatest technique implies absolute mastery and judgment in everything, so that the brilliant fast passage is given with the necessary force and élan, while the soft elegant ornamentation receives in its turn grace and finish. To play rhythmically the pianist must possess technique of finger articulation, to play with colour he must acquire the technique of the pedal, to play with feeling and emotion he must have the technique of touch, to play with power he must learn the technique of how to apply strength. All these many branches go to make up the one comprehensive material called technique which the pianist must work with to produce his æsthetic objective.

Therefore no student may despise or undervalue even its most mechanical aspects. For as in architecture every humble and uninteresting stone has its own indispensable æsthetic necessity in the building of the palace or cathedral, even so is it also in pianoforte playing; to attain the noblest results no details of workmanship, however insignificant, should be neglected.

Genius means not only imagination and temperament, but also the capacity of conveying them to the world through the vehicle of some medium, over which a complete mastery has been obtained.

CHAPTER IV

CAN YOU PLAY A SCALE?

AMONG the many students who come and play to me and ask me for advice, the majority remind me of a well-known limerick about a certain young lady of Rio, whose skill was so scanty she played *Andante* instead of *Allegro con brio!*

I must be excused for drawing attention to the young lady of Rio, but it is because her case is true and typical of so many other young females—and also males—whose houses are much nearer London than Rio. I should like, therefore, to say a few words about attempting to play great masterpieces of pianoforte music without sufficient knowledge of technique, and especially of that immensely important branch of it, the mastery of scales.

It has been my experience that whenever particularly young and raw students come to play to me and want to show what they can do, they invariably attempt such giant works as the Brahms-Handel Variations, or the Appassionata Sonata of Beethoven, or the Chopin Ballads. After they have finished playing a sonata or two (most often in *tempo andante,* like our friend of Rio), I ask them to play me a scale. They usually evince astonishment at my request, and answer that they never practise scales at all.

If ever they do what I ask, their performance of them proves to be, as a rule, unrhythmical, uneven and altogether unsatisfactory. Yet most pianoforte works contain passage-writing which is directly based upon scale progressions. I have known many advanced pianoforte students who are quite unable to arrive at any high standard of performance through lack of technical knowledge and want of proficiency in scale-playing.

EXPRESSION OR EXECUTION?

Who does not quote, at times, in referring to such performers, the hackneyed plea for indulgence: " He makes up in expression what he lacks in execution "? As if this excuse itself did not prove upon examination to be a sheer piece of nonsense. For where there is no sufficient command of execution the expression can only be halting, stilted, and ineffective. In a reproductive art, such as pianoforte-playing, the perfect rendering of all the emotions inspired by the music can only be obtained through unlimited control of technique, which, of course, implies absolute mastery of manual dexterity.

So many talented amateurs who really wish to study their art to the backbone and attain professional proficiency do not realize that they must first acquire what is generally known among artists as a good "school." The world "school" used in this sense means a firm background of technical principles by which difficulties can be solved in the most logical and profitable manner. The acquirement of these principles can only be gained in the years of hard work which should precede any serious attempt at performance.

It was interesting to me, in the light of my views on this subject, to have been present recently at the Dancing School of the Russian Ballet. Here their greatest stars practise every day, for several hours, technical exercises and steps which eventually constitute a wonderful and intricate ballet. And though to the impatient the mere study of scales may seem intolerably dull, yet it is a wonderful feeling to notice power growing gradually, and things becoming easy which at first seemed insurmountable.

PERFECT SCALE-PLAYING

On the piano there are many branches of virtuosity to be mastered, but none more essential than perfect scale-playing. Much of the bad fingering which impedes pianists from getting through passages of elaborate runs is due to ignorance of this important technical detail.

Almost of equal necessity with scales are arpeggi, which should always be practised in conjunction with them, with every kind of different accent and rhythm. The serious student should make a point of studying these for at least one hour every day, playing scales and arpeggi in four different tonalities each day, and going through all their harmonic developments as set down in the compendium at the end of this book.

I believe in practising scales slowly, and playing each hand separately, and, above all, in working with the utmost concentration of the mind. One hour of concentrated practice is worth ten hours of mechanical repetition of difficulties by people who scarcely think what they are doing. Practising, even of scales, must never become mechanical, or the labour is vain.

The student should always be intently listening, and be sure that no single note has an ugly sound, but that each is played with a musical touch and the tone produced is round and full. Even the most uninspiring exercises can be made to sound pleasing and harmonious if played with, scrupulous attention to the quality of tone.

A MENTAL STIMULUS

It is to this end essential in scale-playing that a certain pressure should be given on the keys with every finger as it falls. The importance of this pressure lies not actually in itself, but in the principle it contains. For the action of making the effort of pressure upon each note gives a mental stimulus. This idea of continually renewed pressure to " activate " work is also advocated by some of the professors of physical culture. Springs are made in dumbbells for the hands of victims to press upon. These trainers of the body have realized by experience that unless the minds of their patients can be concentrated on their work by having to press the spring of the dumbbell, their actions soon become purely automatic and cease to exercise their muscles properly.

So it is also on the pianoforte keyboard. The player's mind is kept alert by having to press the fingers down upon the keys, and being thus forced to think about what he is doing. For if the fingers merely run over the keyboard without attention, that kind of practice can do no possible good whatever. The mind must always be present like a general, whilst the fingers are the soldiers who obey his behests.

No doubt every beginner should seek out a good teacher to show him how to set about conquering difficulties, but however wonderful the teacher, it is up to the pupil to concentrate and see that his mind works in conjunction with his fingers. Hard work for the mastery of detail and unlimited concentration of thought are necessary for arriving at any really fine performance on the pianoforte.

A COMMON FAULT

The fault of most players who come to me is that their preparation before attempting to attack a great work has not been sufficient. And for this the teacher must sometimes be held responsible to a certain degree, because, naturally desiring the pupil to make quick progress, he gives him Liszt's Rhapsodies and Beethoven's greatest Sonatas to play, after only a few months of perfunctory study. The students also have a natural desire to astonish their parents and gratify their patrons, and often to justify the spending of a good deal of money on their musical education. Most of them rely on so-called musical feeling, charming touch, and other elusive qualities, which have possibly been " enthused " over by their supporters! Thus they fritter away valuable time in chase of shadows, instead of settling down under a severe and accomplished master to genuine hard study of scales and other exercises.

I am constantly seeing advertisements by teachers of " how to play the piano in five minutes by correspondence! " But I know by my own experience that after thirty years of continuous study there are still many problems in piano-playing that I cannot solve.

SELF-TAUGHT PIANISTS

There certainly are occasional geniuses whose exceptional powers and facilities for the pianoforte enable them to perform in public without having been through the workshop of the technical school. But these are few and far between, and upon inquiring closely about them it will generally be found that their labour and difficulty in mastering technical passages are immeasurably greater than those of other pianists with far less talent who have had the advantage of thorough schooling.

They will most often complain bitterly themselves of the lack of that foundation of technique they never had the opportunity of acquiring, and the want of which continues to hamper them through life. In fact, one of the greatest living pianists, who was practically self-taught, once told me that he would have saved himself ten years of drudgery if he had been able to study one year with a great pianoforte teacher like Leschetitzky.

The hands and movements of such self-taught pianists, too, almost always look ungainly and distorted on the keyboard when playing awkward passages. And this is not only disturbing to the eye but very often also to the quality of the sound, which quickly becomes laboured and heavy under severe strain. The player who " arrives " with such disabilities must indeed have genius for the piano! But there are not many such highly-gifted people in the world, who succeed in spite of every obstacle. I believe the inhabitants of this globe number over fifteen hundred millions, but amongst them all there are not more than a dozen really great pianists!

Therefore, student, learn to play scales carefully, tunefully, exactly, rhythmically, smoothly, and eventually quickly, and arpeggi evenly, clearly, and elegantly before embarking upon the performance of the great works of pianoforte literature. Many cast up their eyes to Heaven in an inspired way while playing, hoping, I suppose, thereby to make up for lack of practice on this earth! But Heaven cannot help them if they have not learned to play scales and arpeggi properly.

N.B.—A compendium of scales, arpeggi, thirds and octaves is given at the end of this book.

CHAPTER V

ELEMENTARY PRINCIPLES FOR STUDY

To arrive at any real result in the study of the piano, it is essential to start very young, and to train both the ear and the hand from childhood. In the case of the beginner, the purely mechanical side of how to hold the hand and produce a supple articulation, is, of course, the main object, but together with this, I am of the opinion that elementary instruction should be given in harmony and the rudiments of music, that the pupil may begin to understand a little about the progressions of sounds and the sense of rhythm which is so necessary to musical development. Nowadays, there are many and various systems of teaching children these elements of music, in forms that will interest and entertain them while they learn almost unconsciously. And such teaching greatly facilitates the technical study, as it makes the child interested in what he is learning, and able to appreciate to a certain extent the difference and gradations of the tones he produces.

Now, as regards the mechanical beginning, without which no one can really play the piano properly, the most important thing is to start with a good method of playing. For there is no doubt that all reliable technique is the outcome of a good common-sense system to begin with. Of course there exists many crankisms about this; the student may go to one teacher who will tell him the only way to play the piano is to sit practising at it from fourteen to fifteen hours a day, just doing finger exercises. He will go to another who will assure him he will only arrive at success if he persists for years, never lifting his fingers more than exactly one-half an inch from the keys!

Again, another will pretend that the only way to learn is by always playing *pianissimo,* another that it is necessary to do exercises only on a table, and never use the keyboard for practising at all, while still another believes in the purely mechanical development of the fingers, by playing hours and hours of scales! Then there are many also who declare that all technique is "Anathema," and that every one should play as nature tells them to!

Perhaps this might occasionally be successful with a natural-born

35

genius, but it would be an exceptionally gifted being who would go very far without any method or school, as we call it, to start with. For the human mind needs, at the outset, the guidance and direction in all the arts of certain elementary rules, born of the amassed experience of the best teachers and thinkers; and the complete assimilation of these rules are the best aids and helps to the attainment of a more perfect self-expression, when the time comes for the individuality of a great talent to assert itself.

FIG. I.   Correct position when seated at the keyboard.

But what is a good method? Why, a common-sense one, surely! And is such a method far to seek? No, undoubtedly not! It must be merely a system which does not exaggerate, and that leaves every part of the hand and arm in a natural easy position. The hand will then look comfortable upon the keyboard, and endless time will be saved in arriving at an easy supple velocity of the fingers. For the terrific labour which is involved by the neglect of these simple principles, in mastering swiftness and lightness of articulation, only those can testify to who have had the bitter experience of bad teaching to start with. I am, therefore, going to give here a few of what I consider the essential points to aim at, when commencing to learn the piano.

POSITION AT THE KEYBOARD

The first thing, then, that presents itself is the position of the body when seated at the instrument. With regard to this, the pupil should be seated with his chair exactly at the middle of the keyboard, and at a medium distance, that is to say, neither too near nor too far, but so that his fingers reach and fall easily and naturally upon the white notes when he is sitting upright on the front half of the chair.

On no account should the pupil be allowed to lean back, but always be seated on the forward portion of his seat. The seat should be sufficiently raised so that the pupil's elbows at their

Fig. 2. Showing cup-like position of the hand.

natural angle will be almost on a level with the keyboard, if anything just a little below it as shown in Fig. 1.

The elbows should be held closely to the body, and the wrist dropped slightly below the keys. Being thus seated, the next matter we come to is settling the position of the hand itself. This should be as follows: The fingers should fall arched upon the keys, the knuckles raised, the wrist just below the keyboard, and the palm of the hand forming a sort of cup as shown on this page (Fig. 2).

It is a very good plan with a beginner, to make him take an apple or a ball of similar size in the palm of the hand, hold it lightly with the fingers spread out round it, and then drop it out of the palm as the hand descends upon the keyboard. The hand will then retain the cup-like position with the fingers spread upon the keys. (See Fig. 2.)

Having thus described what I consider the perfect position of the hand, I will now proceed to explain how to exercise the fingers in order to retain that position, and make it become a habit. This will be arrived at by practising in the following manner: Press the fingers down well arched on to five consecutive white notes, and hold them down altogether. Then lift each finger in turn, holding the others down meanwhile, and strike the key with the lifted finger, taking great care all the time that the hand is perfectly supple and relaxed, and that nothing is stiff. This exercise, done every day for five minutes by each hand separately, will soon give the fingers and hands a perfectly easy and natural position upon the keyboard, and preserve the cup shape of the palm of the hand. (See Exercise No. 1 in compendium at the end of the book.)

A CUP-LIKE POSITION

This acquiring of the cup-like position of the hand will be found enormously useful later on, in the playing of scales and arpeggi, as it allows easy passage of the thumb under the other fingers. In connection with the striking of the keys by the fingers, I would further say that merely putting down the finger and letting it strike with its own weight, is no good, as the sound produced thereby is inadequate and uncontrolled.

My idea is that when lifted, the finger must be brought down with a certain amount of pressure upon the note which is struck. This pressure should be produced from the forearm and transmitted through the fingers to the key, the wrist being all the time absolutely relaxed. Later on, as the student arrives at a higher development of finger technique, the articulation can be exercised purely from the fingers, but in the beginning, in order to acquire a full round tone, the control must be taught from the forearm by means of pressure from that part.

Again, above all, I cannot too much insist upon the necessity for relaxation of the wrist, and the rest of the body, for in it consists, I am convinced, half the secret for obtaining an easy and sure technique. It must also never be forgotten that as the piano is a purely mechanical instrument, the great object must be to produce all gradations of tone without the sound being either forced, harsh or stiff. Moreover, the cardinal principle in the production of such tone is that the body, and especially the wrist, remain in complete relaxation.

Nothing tends so much to hardness of tone on the piano as any rigidity in any part of the body. Also to obtain this most precious quality of flexibility, the articulation of the fingers must be entirely generated by the muscles of the hand, and controlled, as I have already explained as regards force, by the forearm.

FINGER CONTROL

To recapitulate the whole matter and condense it, the principle set up is that all control on the keyboard should be established by the fingers, the hand and the forearm, the wrist remaining entirely supple. This, in my opinion, applies to all finger technique, and is essential for arriving at a completely successful issue.

Care must also be taken not to allow any beating of time by the head or foot, as this may easily degenerate into a nervous trick, and certainly tends to encourage jerky and rigid movements of the body. It is a good plan to make the beginner, after each exercise that he does, lift the hand off the keys and shake it gently from the wrist, so as to ensure that the relaxation is preserved, and that there is no excessive effort or fatigue of the muscles or any cramped action whatsoever. I do not believe in striving to lift the fingers too high off the keys every time when striking each note, because, in a highly complicated mechanical instrument like the piano, every movement must be conserved as much as possible, and naturally any extra effort only tends to lose time, thereby impairing the velocity in fast passages.

Some people think that by teaching that the fingers be lifted very high they can get a clearer and more distinct articulation, but I do not agree with this, as I have always found from my own experience that if the wrist is relaxed, thus allowing absolute freedom to the fingers, they will articulate just as distinctly, and with much added lightness and quality of tone, if not lifted too high.

The most important elemental stage of thus holding the hands in a natural supple position, having been well initiated, by means such as I have just been trying to explain, the pupil will do well to proceed with five-finger exercises of all descriptions, until he has thoroughly mastered the position in question, and it has become a second nature to him to hold his hands thus. With a child beginner of from six to ten, after a month of practising for not more than ten minutes a day, if well watched, the hands, according to my personal experience, should be absolutely in order. The *Five-Finger Exercises* of Hanon are excellent in this respect for settling the fingers in the right way, and also will keep a child interested in the different groups of notes presented. I know of none better for the purpose of elementary practising.

TECHNIQUE IN EXTENDED POSITION

We must pass on from five-finger exercises to the technique of extended positions of the hand, such as are to be found in scales, arpeggi, chords, thirds and octaves. I propose here to speak of scales and arpeggi only, and shall first say a word or two about scales, for which the five-finger exercises I have just been discussing are, of course, merely a preparation. But the great difficulty of scale playing, which consists in learning how to pass the thumb successfully under the other fingers, without causing a break in the continuity of the sound, is absent in five-finger exercises, though through them the student learns the right way of holding the hand on the keyboard, so that it is always ready to do its work when called upon in the scales, and also the fingers are trained to exert the necessary pressure on the key.

BETTER SCALE STUDY

In order to obtain this smooth passage of the thumb in scales, I advise that the wrist always be kept absolutely loose, and that in slow practice, when the thumb is ready to pass, the wrist be raised temporarily from its usually low position to a higher one; also the finger which strikes the last note before the thumb has to pass (in scales it is always the 3rd or 4th finger), should be slightly inclined towards the direction in which the hand is going to travel.

Taking the ascending scale of C major, in the right hand, for example, and illustrating what I want to point out by a diagram thus:

C.	D.	E.	F.	G.	A.	B.	C.
—	—	/	—	—	—	/	—
(1).	2.	3.	(1).	2.	3.	4.	(1).
Thumb.			*Thumb.*				*Thumb.*

→*Ascending right hand.*

It will be seen that upon the E, which is struck by the 3rd finger, the line underneath is raised and inclined towards the direction the hand has to go, so as to represent the lifting up of the wrist, and the inclining of the finger. The thumb then passes easily underneath the fingers on to the next note F, without any awkwardness. The same movement is repeated further up the scale after the 4th finger, and so on through all the octaves in ascending scales for the right hand. For descending scales, the process is reversed. The wrist is raised when the thumb falls, and the finger which follows it is inclined downwards in the direction the hand has to go.

C.	B.	A.	G.	F.	E.	D.	C.
—	—	—	—	/	—	—	/
5.	4.	3.	2.	(1).	3.	2.	(1).
				Thumb.			*Thumb.*

→*Descending right hand.*

In the left hand exactly the same process is used as in the right, only the order is reversed, that is to say, the wrist is raised at the thumb, in the ascending scale, and at the 3rd or 4th finger, in the descending one, the inclining position of the fingers being correspondingly observed. In all scales in every tonality, this action of the wrist and fingers should be similar, and the principle of lifting the wrist at the finger before the thumb passes, and inclining the finger in the direction the hand is to travel, greatly facilitates this passage of the thumb, and ensures smoothness and freedom of motion. In fast scales this movement practically disappears, as exaggerated actions only impede swiftness and look ungainly, but a smooth and undulating motion remains, which is elegant and imparts an elastic and supple articulation, and also gives character to the various passages.

CHAPTER VI

SOME FURTHER HINTS HOW TO MASTER THE
KEYBOARD

SCALES CONTINUED AND ARPEGGI

EVEN TONE is another most difficult object to strive for in playing
scales, for the human hand is physically so constituted that certain
of the fingers are weaker than the others, namely, the 4th and 5th
are the weak ones, and the 1st, 2nd and 3rd the strong ones. From
this fact ensues the natural consequence that the notes struck by
the 1st, 2nd and 3rd fingers are liable to be louder and firmer in tone
than those upon which 4th and 5th fall.

This weakness can only be corrected by pressure from the forearm transmitted to the fingers, as I have already insisted upon when
speaking of the articulation in five-finger exercises. The pressure
is here used as an equalizer, in this fashion, that the conscious habit
of the pressure having been established by practice, it works upon
the mind and forces the performer unconsciously to give an extra
compensative pressure to the weaker fingers, according as he detects
by his ear that they require it.

This equalizing of the tone by pressure serves again to illustrate
how the theory of its administration through the forearm, working
upon the fingers, establishes absolute control of the muscles, not so
much by its direct action on the fingers as by its indirect stimulus to
the mind, which through it becomes conscious that it has work to do,
and is alert to command the muscles properly.

Later on it will be seen how vital a part of piano technique this
control of the muscles by the mind is, constituting, as it does, the
principle upon which is based the imparting of light and shade,
gradations of expression and *tempo,* in fact the life which changes
the sounds of the mechanical instrument into music.

Scales should be played every day and in all tonalities. Upon the
black notes the fingers may be slightly extended, as it will be found
difficult to keep them quite as rounded as on the white ones, owing
to the lack of space. Finally, it is important in practising scales that

they should be played absolutely correctly, therefore it is always best to practise each hand separately.

ARPEGGI

In some ways smoothness is even more difficult to master in arpeggi than in scales, as in them the intervals necessitate wide jumps, which have to be negotiated. I will take the arpeggio in the common chord of C major in the right hand, to illustrate first the method which I.have found very successful with students.

Right hand ascending. →

C.	E.	G.	C.	E.	G.	C.
—	—	/	—	—	/	—
(1).	2.	3.	(1).	2.	3.	(1).
Thumb.			*Thumb.*			*Thumb.*

The idea is the same as in the scale. The problem which presents itself is how to smooth over the jump between G and C. On the accompanying diagram I attempt to show, by the small lines under-

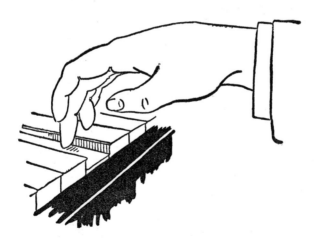

FIG. 3. Showing the 3rd finger placed with raised wrist for passage of thumb.

neath the notes, how the finger which falls just before the thumb (in this case it is the 3rd, on G) is raised from the wrist and inclined towards the direction to which the hand has to proceed.

This 3rd finger should be placed upon the note exactly one and three-quarter inches length away from the edge of the key towards the back of the keyboard, and the thumb should fall underneath it upon C, just the length of its own nail away from the key edge, that is about a quarter of an inch. Thus:

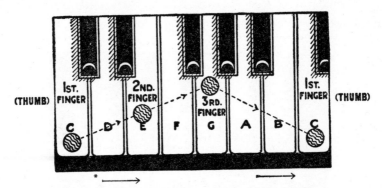

FIG. 4. *Arpeggio. C major. Right hand ascending,*
showing relative positions of the thumb and finger.

Coming down the position is reversed, as follows: The thumb falls upon the note at the one and three-quarter-inch position from the edge of the key, when it is lifted up by the wrist movement, and the 3rd or 4th finger, as the case may be, then falls over the thumb on to the note below, about one-quarter inch from the edge of the key. Thus:

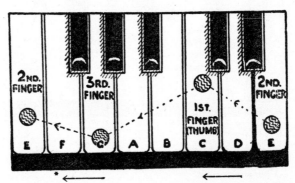

FIG. 5. *Arpeggio. C major. Right hand descending*
(starting from right of diagram), beginning with 2nd finger on E, so as to show relative position of the fingers used.

The movement of the wrist makes for smoothness at the jump and helps to prepare the hand for the next position. The principle

*Arrows show direction.

is similar in both hands as in the scales, only reversed in the left; that is to say, when the left hand ascends the thumb is lifted by the wrist and placed one and a quarter inches from the end of the key, while going down it is the 3rd or 4th finger which assumes that position, the thumb falling on the key at the quarter inch from the end of the key, as in the ascending right hand arpeggio.

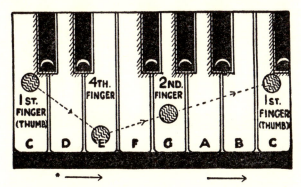

FIG. 6. *Arpeggio. C major. Left hand ascending* (starting from left of diagram), beginning with the *thumb* on C, so as to show the relative positions of the other fingers.

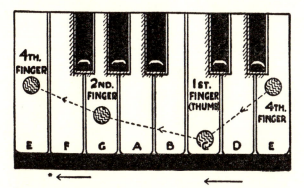

FIG. 7. *Arpeggio. C major. Left hand descending* (starting from right of diagram), beginning with the 4th finger on E, so as to show the relative position of the fingers used.

Exactly the same rules apply in all the varieties of arpeggio playing.

It is absolutely imperative for students who wish to acquire any proficiency in pianoforte playing to practise a good amount of scales and arpeggi every day as given at the end of this book, for these

* Arrows show direction.

difficulties are the A B C of the piano, without which no one can get on. *Therefore, he who* starts his work regularly and thoroughly every morning with a course of scales and arpeggi will gradually find a fine easy technique coming to him and a mastery over the keyboard which will be of inestimable advantage to him when he starts investigating the treasure house of pianoforte literature.

CHAPTER VII

ADVANCED TECHNIQUE: THIRDS, SIXTHS AND OCTAVES

I PROPOSE here to discuss briefly the higher or advanced technique of pianoforte playing as is to be found in the study of Thirds, Sixths and Octaves. Of course this is really a highly complicated subject about which innumerable books and treatises have been written without nearly exhausting all the material for discussion to which it gives rise. But the few remarks that I am going to make now are chiefly intended for the practical help of working students, and I shall confine myself more or less to explaining one or two of the methods which I personally find useful in mastering the difficulties that occur in these complex stages of virtuosity. For as modern pianoforte technique requires great development of double note playing and such-like independence of the fingers, so it must be the aim of every student to discover the easiest and shortest cuts which may bring him to proficiency in this branch of his art.

A MELODIC OUTLINE

To commence then with the study of passages in thirds:—A great many people seek to play these in what I term a "player-pianistic style" instead of a "pianistically plastic" one. By this I mean that they make a point of striking both the notes that compose thirds together with exactly the same pressure of tone, thus giving no doubt an absolutely mechanical precision to double note progressions, but thereby taking away from them, in my opinion, all their melodic character and charm. For I maintain that all passage playing, whether it be in thirds, sixths, or single notes, should necessarily preserve a melodic outline, otherwise it degenerates into mere sequences of notes for the display of agility and loses every musical significance.

For whereas some regard elaborate passages as entirely mechanical embellishments, the earnest musician will realize that this is not often the case; on the contrary, close analysis will almost always prove them to be intricate and reasoned embroideries of melody.

47

Now in single note passages it is easy to obtain some sort of musical contour, because the brain has only one line to develop. But with double notes this is all far more complicated, especially as the melodic ideal remains to be achieved here, just as much as in the simpler case. And hard enough as it is to accomplish satisfactory results with only one finger to think of, what is to be done when two are having to be managed at once?

USE MENTAL CONCENTRATION

Well, I will start from the first third in the scale of C major, which will be C and E. Next come D and F, and in attempting to pass rapidly from the first third to the second one a difficulty will be immediately encountered. This is the ungovernable tendency of each finger to run apart from each other, and refuse to pull together at all. A purely mental difficulty though is this, and it can be overcome by training the mind, and accustoming it to govern the hands and fingers in complete independence one of the other. In fact I am convinced that in general, technical facility and control can only be obtained by great mental concentration, and not merely through mechanical practice.

That is why some people are able to learn to play a scale in thirds in an hour quite decently, because they possess the necessary power of brain, while others who may have quite as much musical talent will never master one at all though they work six hours a day at it! I do not mean to say by this that thirds do not require an enormous amount of study, because of course they do, only to be successful the practice must be accompanied by much concentrated brain effort. Therefore one of the principal efforts of a good pianoforte teacher should be to stimulate in every possible manner the mental faculties of his pupils.

Thirds should be worked with pressure of the finger on the top note, that is to say, in the third of C and E the pressure should be on the E, in the third of D and F on the F, and so on up the scale. (See Fig. 9.) In continuing the scale, after having struck C, with the 1st finger or thumb (taking the right hand ascending), the finger is raised and D is approached with the 2nd finger. The 1st finger on the C is taken off very abruptly, almost as if it was on a spring hinge, whilst the top note E is held by the 3rd finger, which becomes slightly stiffened and is kept down after the lower one has been raised. (See Figs. 10 and 11.) The bottom note of the third might almost be ¾ of the value of the top note by the way it should be released, practically equivalent to the following example:

FIG. 8. Example to show holding on of top note in Third Scales after lower note has been released.

though it will not be distinguishable in the sound of the rhythm. This method is, of course, only for slow practice; the action will disappear in fast *tempi,* but what will remain is a clearness of outline on the upper notes of the thirds, which is the object to be achieved. The wrist should be held higher than in ordinary scales, where it is kept low, except at the passage of the thumb. But by holding the

FIG. 9. Position of hand upon commencement of Third Scales.

wrist somewhat elevated in third scales, it ensues that the pressure of the top fingers is accentuated.

Although it be held higher than in single note scales, the wrist must still be kept absolutely relaxed, and the pressure must be obtained through the forearm acting direct upon the fingers. When the 5th finger is arrived at, it should be placed on the key on the side or ball of the finger, the wrist being meanwhile raised even a little more, and the hand inclined in the direction upwards to which it is proceeding. (See Fig. 12.)

Descending, a similar inclined position is taken by the thumb. (See Fig. 13.)

In the left hand it is the thumb in the ascending scale, and the 5th finger in the descending one which assumes the position.

FIG. 10. Position showing the raising of the lower finger whilst the upper one is slightly stiffened and held on.

At the end of this chapter on page 60 I give what I find the best fingering to be used for simple third scales, and also for chromatic scales in thirds.

PRACTISING SCALES IN SIXTHS

Passages in sixths are extremely complicated and are rarely to be met with, as they necessitate so much extension of the hand, and it is consequently difficult to play them *legato* at all. The general principle for playing sixths is the same as that for thirds, but it is not advisable to practise them a great deal, because the continued extension of the position may prove injurious to the hand, and strain or cramp can result.

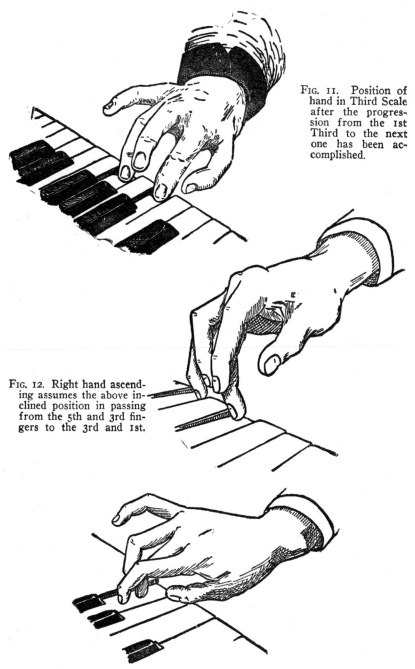

Fig. 11. Position of hand in Third Scale after the progression from the 1st Third to the next one has been accomplished.

Fig. 12. Right hand ascending assumes the above inclined position in passing from the 5th and 3rd fingers to the 3rd and 1st.

Fig. 13. Right hand descending, showing inclined position of the hand when passing down from the thumb and 3rd fingers to the 5th and 3rd.

THE PRACTICE OF OCTAVES

I now come to Octave Technique for which every sort of studies have been and continue to be written. Now the real octave wrist, combining great strength with high nervous tension and suppleness, is a gift of nature, like the capacity for playing *staccato* bowing on the violin. But those who do not possess the power can develop it to a limited extent. There are several methods of playing octaves, one being with a loose wrist and the 5th finger slightly stiffened. This is a good way for octaves in a slow *tempo,* but when speed is required it can only be secured by nervous contraction of the arm, the wrist being kept stiff meanwhile. To accomplish this needs much muscular strength, as the advantage of the loose wrist has to be discarded, and whenever the rapidity of the *tempo* increases, the stiffening of the wrist must increase also.

As far as the practice of octaves go, I do not think merely playing them in scales is efficacious, and, as I have already said, there are so many studies devised on this most difficult branch of piano technique that it is best to work with them. Those of Kullak are, I find, especially excellent. It is very unwise ever to work at octave playing for more than ten minutes at a time, as it is so fatiguing and may injure the arm if overdone. But there are ways of helping oneself to relieve exhaustion during long sequences of octaves. Some of these devices are useful for all, though generally each player finds out means for himself according to the structure of his own particular muscles.

To illustrate what I mean by these helps against fatigue, I will give an example from the A flat Polonaise of Chopin. The great octave passage in the second part for the left hand lasts 34 bars, which is a tremendous length, as all pianists know, and the strain may become almost unbearable.

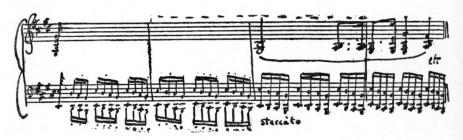

FIG. 14. Extract from the A flat Polonaise of Chopin, showing Octave passage in left hand, which lasts 34 bars.

Here it is a considerable relief to think of the passage as in a semi-circular motion from left to right.   Thus:

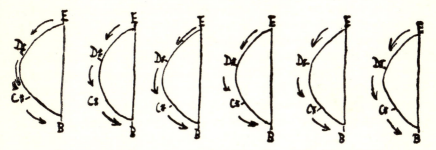

FIG. 15.   Diagram illustrating the mental device of placing each group of four Octaves as component parts of half a circle.

Again, in the enormously difficult octave passage for the right hand in the Sixth Rhapsody of Liszt, it will be found to be of assistance to keep changing the position of the wrist from being high to becoming low.   Thus:

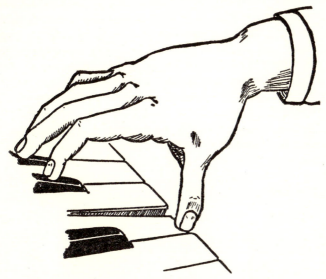

FIG. 16.   First position of hand with wrist held high in Octave playing.

This very small action of the wrist gives respite for a second from the tension, and sets the momentum of the nervous contraction going again.   (See Fig. 17.)   This same movement can apply to most continuous octave sequences of any length, provided they are in scale-like progressions, or in the form of reiteration. But for octaves which move in arpeggi, this same action would not answer, because here the mind has to be occupied with the matter of judging

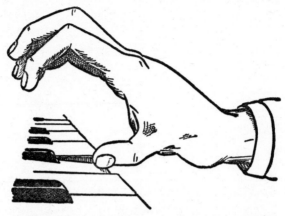

FIG. 17. Second position of hand in Octave playing, with wrist held low to give relief from fatigue.

the distances, or I should rather say, feeling them. For all jumps are very uncertain quantities, and no eye judgment can be possible where a high rate of speed has to be obtained. Therefore in arpeggio-like octave passages only a mental device will be of any

FIG. 18. Extract from "Hungarian Fantasie" of Liszt, showing difficult Octave passages.

The lower bridging lines indicate the mental measurement of the Octave passages in Triplets. The upper lines indicate the 2/4 time in which the sound of the rhythm must proceed undisturbed.

help in the difficulty. This contrivance is to imagine the octaves in groups of threes in the mind, no matter what the rhythm is in which they are written. I take an example out of the Hungarian Fantasie of Liszt for piano and orchestra to show the idea.

It must always be remembered, of course, that the device is only a creation of the imagination and must in no wise be allowed to become evident or interfere with the proper rhythm. But as a mental measurement it will always facilitate the negotiating of rapid jumps correctly and continuously. The last passage in the Concerto in C minor of Saint-Saëns for piano and orchestra, also serves to illustrate the method of reducing the difficulty by this calculation of the mind. (See Fig. 19.)

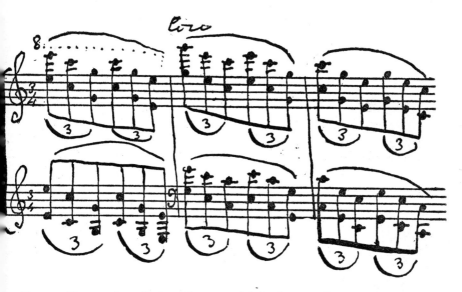

Fig. 19. Passage from C minor Concerto of Saint-Saëns to illustrate the mental device of considering the Octaves in groups of threes, as indicated by the lines below, though the sound of the rhythm must remain in 3/4 time.

Still more hard than so-called simple octave technique is that where intermediate notes between the octaves have to be struck together with them, as in successive progression of rapid chords, such as are to be found in the opening cadenza of Liszt's E flat Concerto. (See Fig. 23, p. 57.) This starts with a tremendous sequence of grand chords in C major, which is extremely difficult to play accurately, and can only be mastered by unceasing practice. In such a passage the wrist should be kept loose and the intermediate notes (in the chord of C major it is the second finger on G) should be struck with rather a stiff finger, so as to form a sort of point of support, the thumb and 5th fingers, however, falling loosely on the two octave notes, C and Octave C.   The hand should be arched and form a cup-like position. Thus:

FIG. 20.   Showing position of hand when playing
Octaves with intermediate notes.

The stiffening of the intermediate finger must be very slight and almost imperceptible; in fact, here again it should be little more than a mental impression.   I give the fingering which I use in the afore-mentioned passage in chords out of the Liszt concerto, in the hope that it may help some who may be struggling with that particular cadenza.   (See Fig. 23, p. 57.)

For very rapid octave scales with intermediate notes, it is of assistance, instead of striking the middle note with the finger in its natural position, which interferes here with speed, to strike it upon the key with the first phalange joint of the finger, as in the following passage out of Saint-Saëns' C minor Concerto. Thus:

FIG. 21.   Showing intermediate note taken with phalange
joint to help speed.

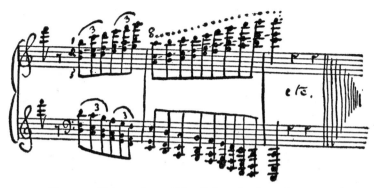

FIG. 22. Extract from Saint-Saëns' C minor Concerto.

The above is a passage where the intermediate notes between the Octaves can be struck with the whole of the first phalange joint of the finger instead of with the tip of the finger simply. This is a device for facilitating speed, and can only be used in the right hand.

But this last is a technical hint for helping rapidity, to be used only by those who have already reached a considerable stage of virtuosity and also possess a wide stretch of the hand, and it should in no case be adopted by the student even of advanced technique! I merely mention it as a curious instance of the little ingenuities that can make the greatest difficulties become possible.

What are termed broken octaves are also continually to be met with, especially in adaptations of pieces from orchestral scores and in the works of Beethoven and Mozart. These have to be played with great skill if they are to sound really well and make a good

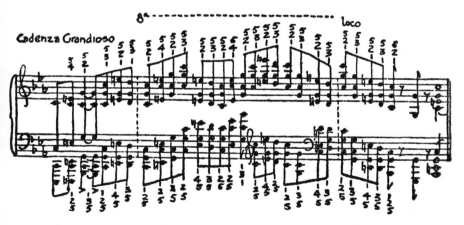

FIG. 23. Extract from Liszt's Concerto in E flat, showing fingering of opening Cadenza.

effect, therefore they must be patiently studied. For practising them I advise using the 1st and 5th fingers with equal strength, the wrist being kept stiff and the hand oscillating to and fro as if it and the fingers were made of one piece with the forearm. There are excellent studies for the development of broken octave technique in Czerny's "Kunstfertigkeit."

INDIVIDUAL CHORD PLAYING

And now for a few words about individual chord playing, as it is so important to discover the right way to produce a fine and noble sound when striking these. The first essential here is to find how to obtain strength without hardness of touch. Strength there must be, of course, tempered by judgment, for without it the pianist will be unable to give out enough and graduating increase of tone when necessary. For especially in a dramatic piece where one often meets with an ever-growing crescendo of tone culminating upon a given point, if the performer lacks accumulative force he cannot achieve this effect, and so the piece may end in an anti-climax and the whole artistic meaning of the work be missed.

Now one way to produce strength of tone is to throw the hands down on the chords by lifting them high above the keys before striking. I do not advocate this, as it is so uncertain, and disaster may easily overtake the player at any moment by his falling upon the wrong notes. For it needs great precision of eye to strike many notes together correctly from a height.

How, then, can extra force be applied without sacrificing the accuracy of notes or the tone quality? With abrupt chords I find the following method efficacious, namely, a quick contraction of the forearm, accompanied by an action of the fingers, as though they were trying to dig themselves into the keys.

For final chords at the end of a great passage, the same digging of the fingers and contraction of the forearm should be supplemented by a motion of the hand turning round upon the notes with a sort of jerk, as if it was trying to lock or unlock a key in a door. The fingers at the same time having finished their digging action should contract slightly towards the palm of the hand. Passages ending with a single note that has to be struck with great power or vehemence can also be manipulated by this same action of the hand, which I call the "lock-the-door motion." It is most effective in adding extra strength when necessary, and even in *pianissimo* chords, where distinctive accent is required, it will be found to apply successfully, though with these, of course, the turning and contraction of the hand will only amount to a slight pressure abruptly administered.

In general, I advise that with all chord playing, whether in abrupt individual cases or in successions of *legato* chords, the strength and volume of tone should be produced by concentrated pressure from the forearm. For thereby will the pianist draw from his instrument a deep and resonant sound, and avoid hard blows that recall the wood and iron elements of its constitution which it should always be his first aim to make his audience forget.

See Tables of Scales in Thirds on next page.

SCALES IN THIRDS WITH FINGERINGS MARKED

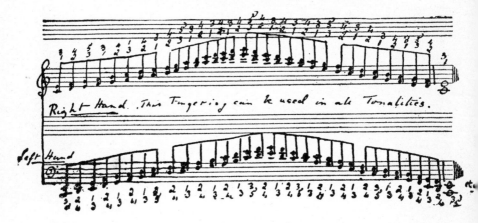

CHROMATIC THIRDS

CHAPTER VIII

ON FINGERING AND MEMORY

CORRECT fingering is a very essential part of piano playing, for it not only conduces to an easy supple technique and to the proper performance of the music, but it also assists in giving light and shade to passages.

This is because some of the fingers are stronger by nature, and some are weaker, and by using them according to their different strength when required, a certain natural gradation of tones is thereby generated.

In the early days of pianoforte playing it was considered wrong to use the thumb or the 5th finger at all upon the keyboard, and later when these two were admitted it was still forbidden by teachers to take a black key with the thumb, and this even until quite a short time ago.

The reason that the use of the thumb was thus limited was partly due to the fact of its working rather awkwardly on the black notes owing to its construction. But the main objection to it really was that it was impossible to get a *legato* tone on the black keys if the thumb was employed. This would be so still if it were not for the help of the pedal; but until recently the pedal had not reached the perfection of mechanism which it now enjoys, and was consequently not applied so much. At any rate people did not think of using it to facilitate the free employment of the thumb. Nowadays, of course, even jumps can be bound over by the skilful application of the pedal, and a smooth, flowing, continuity of tone can be obtained in the most awkward passages.

NATURAL TECHNIQUE

Pianoforte technique might almost be said to be divided into two schools.

The one seems as if it were exactly adapted to suit the peculiar powers of the instrument, and is that which, having been greatly modernized by Chopin, culminated in the genius of Liszt. The passage writing of both these pre-eminent composers for the piano are unsurpassed as pure pianoforte technique both as regards expression, effectiveness and brilliancy.

The other school, on the contrary, could almost be described as having developed on lines antagonistic to the piano's natural limitations and even to those of the human hand. Some of the finest pianoforte works, however, are to be found in this category, two of its greatest representatives being Schumann and Brahms. (It must be remembered that I am speaking here entirely from the point of view of purely mechanical technique, and not considering the musical side of the question at all.)

This is why many of the pianoforte compositions of Schumann, and especially also of Brahms, are so terribly difficult to master. Brahms never seemed to stop to consider much about the limitations of the instrument he was writing for, but let his imagination and creative faculty develop unhindered, and undeterred, by questions of technical unsuitability. Thus some of his most beautiful passages are written almost in defiance of the natural technique of the piano, so that the pianist, in order to arrive at investing them with their full significance and effect, would often be glad of twenty fingers to play them with instead of the mere ten which he possesses!

In this kind of music, tending as it does more towards orchestral effects than to purely pianistic ones, the player must often resort to fingering that at first seems against all reason, to obtain the mastery over the difficulties. For though in general in all piano playing the principle should be firmly established that the hand must look natural and elegant to the eye upon the keyboard, yet here that rule must be thrown overboard, in order to preserve the necessary expression and plasticity.

MY METHOD

There are countless methods of fingering, and most pianists discover for themselves certain particular combinations to specially fit their own hands.

My method is to finger any given passage by starting with the thumb on the first note of the passage, irrespective of whether any of the notes are black or white keys. I then use up the fingers, that is to say, 2, 3, 4, 5, as they naturally fall within the contour of the passage. But as the passage deploys under the hand, I substitute the strongest for the weakest fingers upon the notes which those weak ones would take in the ordinary course of succession. The strongest fingers should be selected on the strong beats of a passage, and the weaker ones on the weak beats, thus producing natural light and shade. The strong fingers are the 1st, 2nd and 3rd; the weakest of them all is the 4th, the 5th being somewhat stronger than the 4th. If by natural sequence it becomes advisable to take the 4th finger it should be preceded wherever possible by the 1st or 2nd finger, as this arrangement will enable it to strike with more power. Thus:

FIG. 24. Extract from Chopin's Ballade in A flat showing substitution of strong for weak fingers.

The fingering above is as usually played without substitution of strong for weak fingers. Lower fingering eliminates the 4th finger completely, thus substituting the strong for the weaker.

In passages where there are big intervals between the successive notes, I use whichever fingers fall easiest within the radius of each gap.

FIG. 25. Concerto in D minor of Rubinstein.

It is not always possible to start a passage with the 1st finger, on account of what has gone before, but when this is the case the next best finger can be employed, and can be proceeded from upon the same basis, using up the fingers that come nearest to the starting finger.

I make no distinction between the white and black keys whatever, but employ the fingers alike on both kinds of notes.

To illustrate the using of the thumb upon the black keys I give here an example from Rubinstein's Concerto in D minor. (See Fig. 25.)

Now as to *the fingering of trills,* some pianists play these by using the two fingers next to each other in succession; but I find that the better way is to employ the 1st and 3rd together in trilling, or the 2nd and 4th, or 3rd and 5th, as the case may present itself, as in the example given below. (See Fig. 26.)

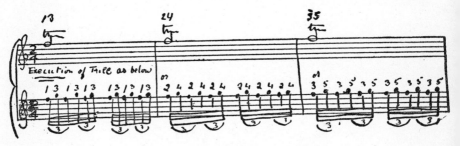

FIG. 26. The Fingering of Trills.

This mode of fingering trills gives velocity and smoothness with the minimum of effort. There are pianists who change the fingers frequently while trilling, as in the example given in Fig. 27, page 52. But I do not find that this repeated moving of fingers produces either smoothness or extra rapidity, in fact I do not advocate its use, and in any case it would not be possible where the trill lay between a black and a white key.

FIG. 27. Frequent changes of fingers during trills which I do not advocate.

When practising trills, it is best to start slowly in triplet time and gradually increase the speed until the requisite rapidity combined with an even articulation can be attained.

Great technicians are always inventing new methods of fingering for difficult progressions, in order to try and make them easier and quicker of mastery. One of comparatively recent origin is for playing chromatic scales in thirds as follows: Slide the 2nd finger from black note to white one, thus using that finger twice running; for instance, proceed from the third D sharp–F sharp taken with the 2nd and 3rd fingers, to the third E–G taken with the 2nd and 4th. I give on page 60 an illustration to show more clearly what is meant. This fingering is a great help to clearness of articulation in chromatic third scales, which clearness, moreover, is always so difficult to obtain in double-note passage playing.

THE BEST GUIDE

It can be safely said that the very best guides for the right application of fingering are to be found in the different scales and

FIG. 28. Extract from Prelude in D flat (Chopin), showing substitution of fingers in *legato* passages.

arpeggi of every kind, which form the basis of all pianoforte technique. For every passage is primarily made on the principles of these progressions, and therefore if students apply the fingering as given especially in my Compendium which deals with Scales and Arpeggio Exercises, they will easily be able with these as a guide to finger correctly most kinds of passages they may find in their pieces.

They may, of course, have to make certain modifications in places upon the lines I have just pointed out in my remarks on the different strength of the fingers, etc., and also because they will have to discover what suits their individual hands best. For it is only reasonable that a hand which can easily stretch the length of twelve notes must needs finger differently from the one that can only reach the distance of six with difficulty! The latter, it is hardly necessary to say, is at a disadvantage, as he has to change fingers so much more frequently than the former with his superior length of hand.

A device which helps to promote a good *legato* tone is to quickly change the fingers from 5 to 1, or from 1 to 5, on the same note while still holding it down, so as to be ready to proceed to the next note without a break in the sound; but this can only be used when the *tempo* is of a very moderate speed.

This substitution of fingers is a very effective way of producing *legato* octaves without using the pedal at all, but it is only possible for hands with a long elastic stretch. Sometimes it may be advisable to divide a passage so that it is spread over both hands, if by so doing greater brilliancy, rapidity or smoothness can be obtained.

In general, unless such a disposition of the passage is specially marked by the composer, its use must be left to the discretion of the teacher or the ingenuity of the student. For there can be no fixed rule about the employment of such divisions; expediency and successful effect are the motives for their introduction.

HINTS ON MEMORY

Correct fingering is also a help to memory. And memory is a most important asset to the modern pianist, as it is now the fashion for him to have to play everything in public by heart. It will, therefore, not be out of place here, if after speaking about fingering I now turn to consider a few points in connection with the faculty of memory.

For the pianist, then, especially, will memory always be a serious study as he has so much to remember at once, and often it is of such a complicated nature. Also he must be of much greater accuracy in his memory than, for instance, the singer or the actor. For the actor can often substitute one word for another without unduly disturbing the sense, while the singer has the accompaniment to support and remind him if he forgets for a moment. But with the pianist everything depends on the correctness of the text, both from the standpoint of his getting through his performance, and from that of the enjoyment of his audience.

Now the more logical the composition is, the easier it is to learn by heart. Therefore the works of Bach and Beethoven are never so hard to remember as those of the modern composers such as Debussy, Ravel, Scriabine, etc. The former, being built up on general principles of structural symmetry that quickly impress themselves on the brain, are much easier to memorize than the latter, that depend more on atmosphere and harmonic colouring and therefore possess a less definite outline to fix in the mind.

Most people have their own way of learning by heart on the piano. I myself find it is a good plan to look upon memory as divided into three distinct parts of the same faculty, each one being able to supplement the others in case of lapse or failure of one of them. These three I distinguish severally as the Harmonic, the Ocular, and the Mechanical memories.

THREE DIVISIONS

The Harmonic memory is that which comes from acquiring the knowledge of the combinations of sounds, development of progressions, modulations, and general musical construction of a composition. This kind of memory can be obtained by dissecting the music into so many periods, subdividing it into harmonic sections, figuring out the various changes of tonality and thus stamping upon the mind a clear perception of the form of the music.

The Ocular or Visual memory is generated by the impression made on the brain by the written pages of music as transmitted to it by the eyes. These get accustomed to seeing the various notes and lines in certain places on the pages, and in definite dispositions in the different periods of the piece, and the reflection of their vision on the inner eye of the brain remains after the actual visible written page of music has been removed.

The third kind of memory, the Mechanical one, comes from the fingers, which from continual mechanical practice and repetition of passages during study, take the habit of playing the groups and progressions of notes almost unconsciously. This last is certainly the most unreliable of the three memories; because, if by inadvertence the pianist takes only once in a passage a different finger from the one his hand is accustomed to, it may put him completely out, and a breakdown can ensue if he has not got the other memories to aid him to retrieve his momentary lapse.

Therefore, like everything mechanical, this finger memory is not to be solely depended upon without the help of the other two, in fact I call it sometimes the Auxiliary memory only. In any case, whichever of the three modes of memory fail, the others can come to the rescue, therefore all three must be cultivated as much as possible.

LEARN BIT BY BIT

It is advisable for the purpose of memorizing, as well as for the general mastery of a piece, to learn it bit by bit, taking eight bars or so at a time. Constant reiteration is bad, for it only fatigues the brain without producing the requisite impression. It is better to play something once or twice over, carefully noticing each detail and then stop to digest it. A good way is to learn each hand's part separately by heart so as to visualize it mentally with such distinctness that the student can, if required, play any given bar by itself and be able to commence unhesitatingly at any point in a piece when asked to do so. Sometimes it is effective to study a piece in the evening, then go to bed and think the music over mentally, note by note, and chord by chord, as if really performing it, and afterwards sleep.

Having done this, the student, upon going fresh to work next morning, will often find that the new piece of the evening before returns clearly to his mind as if it was already a familiar old friend.

No one need be downhearted if the power of learning by heart does not come immediately. For nearly everybody can obtain it in a considerable degree by training, though some people no doubt have a natural talent for it that scarcely seems to need exercising at all to keep it vigorous. Certainly the pianist who possesses by nature a good memory and has also trained it carefully can arrive at the most incredible rapidity in learning music by heart. To wit, Van Bulow, the great pianist, of whom the story is told that he learnt the whole of Tchaikovsky's Variations in F Major for the piano in the train between St. Petersburg and Moscow, and played them by heart at a concert the same evening when he arrived!

No doubt the more musical talent a man possesses, the easier he will learn music by heart, and the longer he will retain it. It is equally certain that temperament, though one of the greatest enhancements of talent, is to some extent prejudicial to reliability of memory during public performance in the following way. The temperamental player loses himself in the beauty of his music. He imagines that he is improvising, he feels as if what he is playing is really the expression of his own soul. Suddenly the dream vanishes! He awakes to actuality and finds that he is still playing a certain part of a set piece by a certain composer! He is perhaps bewildered by the sudden cold douche of consciousness. He realizes his surroundings, he falters, he forgets what comes next!

Rubinstein, greatest of pianists, suffered terribly from this kind of lapse of memory, which he put down entirely to being carried away by his temperament. Still, better the temperament of Rubinstein than the exactitude of the pianola! However, the student is not by any manner of means a Rubinstein, and what was forgiven to his commanding genius cannot be conceded to the ordinary mortal! Therefore the temperamental player will find in his public performance that memory will generally be a source of anxiety to him. But this anxiety ought to be more than compensated for by the reflection that memory can be acquired by patience and reasoning power, while true temperament can never be even simulated, but is a gift of God. The music of Bach is most admirably adapted for developing a precise memory. For in his compositions are to be found the most complicated forms of polyphonic writing, where the mind must be always on the alert to distinguish the many different parts with each their individual workings.

CHAPTER IX

SOME COMMON MISTAKES AND ADVICE HOW TO AVOID
THEM

WHEN a student comes to play to the artist with whom he desires
to study, how often does he ask, when he has finished his performance: " Master, what I really want you to tell me is, whether
I have any very serious faults in my playing? "

Serious faults in his playing! Poor fellow! He probably has
several which he has not yet discovered himself, and which most
likely no one has ever drawn his attention to.

What, then, are some of the most common faults, and at the
same time some of the worst of those which students of the piano
may fall into unsuspectingly through careless tuition? Well, these
are many and various, and are generally very difficult to eradicate.
Moreover, they beset the most talented players, just as much as their
less gifted brethren.

WRONG USE OF PEDAL

To begin with, there is no more usual failing, or one more
damaging to good piano-playing, than too much use of the pedal,
and its application in the wrong places. The pedal is really a
very dangerous attraction to the inexperienced and yet enthusiastic
performer. It is such an alluring temptation to hear the notes
welling into one another, also the blur of sound produced by much
pedalling covers up so many deficiencies of execution.

There is no doubt that the pedal carries with it a sort of special
glamour of its own, so that even children when they first start
learning the piano are always clamouring to be allowed to play
with the pedal. It is their greatest ambition. Yet bad use of the
pedal is quite capable of completely marring the effect of what
might otherwise be a fine rendering of a piece of music. The
pedal should be used to enhance, but never to cover up, and should
be regarded as a means for producing certain definite tone-effects
and variations of tone-colour at precise moments, and not as a
sort of general mist of hot vapour or steam by which each note,
passage and chord becomes enveloped.

Misuse of the pedal is a horrible fault, and can affect great and

70

small alike; it should be carefully guarded against. Indeed, the state it produces on the mind of the listener is similar to that which overheated air creates in the lungs, namely, fatigue, nausea, lassitude, and even, alas, drowsiness!

ANOTHER BLUNDER

Now comes along the temperamental student, burning with ardour for the beauty of the music, longing to make the noble

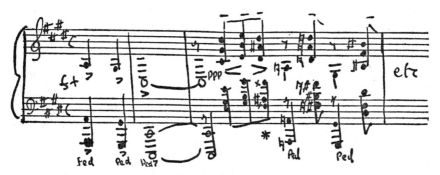

FIG. 29. Prelude in C Sharp minor. S. Rachmaninoff, Op. 3, No. 2.

Examples showing (above) an excerpt from the Prelude in C sharp minor of Rachmaninoff, as written by the composer, and (below) as often played by enthusiasts with the right hand striking each note in the first two bars a fraction after the left. In the third bar of the lower example the chords will be seen arpeggioed instead of together, and again the right hand coming in after the left in the last two chords.

FIG. 30. Prelude in C Sharp minor. S. Rachmaninoff, Op. 3, No. 2.

chords of some fine melody speak out its message! What special pitfall lies ready to entrap his zealous endeavours? Why, in his enthusiasm that the melody in both hands should be properly brought out, he gets one hand playing after the other! Only a fraction of a second after the left hand does the right hand strike, but in that loss of simultaneousness of sound the whole grandeur after which the performer is striving will be dispelled in the irritating effect of one part of the harmony always reaching the ear at a slight interval after the other. This is a most frequent failing amongst very musical people who enjoy tremendously what they are playing; and especially does it occur with them in slow movements, when they will arpeggio the chords between the two hands so much that it sounds to me like drawling in speech, or even like stuttering. These enthusiasts lose their sense of the symmetry of the sound in their intense pleasure over its component parts, and it is hard that the very virtue that lies in their love of the music can thus lead them into danger.

Dragging the time, another tiresome error of judgment, proceeds generally from the same cause of over-fervour. The player who suffers from this blemish mostly owes it to a lack of sense of proportion and taste, and to a certain want of artistic perception of the guiding line between true sentiment and sentimentality.

HURRYING THE *TEMPO*

Hurrying the tempo is nearly as bad, and is sometimes caused by nervousness, though indifference, want of confidence, and the very general mistake of looking upon a *crescendo* as an *accellerando* also give rise to it. People who are inclined to be nervous when playing before others often get a queer kind of defiant sensation when technically difficult passages hover in sight; the "let's get it over and be done with it" sort of feeling, which makes them hurry in an extraordinary manner.

Of course, hurrying may just as well arise from a lack of instinct for rhythm in the student. Where this is the case, it is rather a hopeless look-out, as it is so hard to inculcate a real feeling for rhythm into someone who is not naturally endowed with it. But it has often been my experience to listen to students who were gifted with a most highly-developed sense of rhythm, and yet who hurried, especially over their technically difficult passages, until I began to get positively breathless. This kind of increasing the speed was, of course, due to want of nervous control.

FAULTY RHYTHM

As hurrying and also dragging the *tempi* are both errors connected somewhat with *faulty rhythm,* I will speak of this next as a highly unsatisfactory failing. Rhythm is no doubt to a great extent instinctive, and is bound up a good deal with individual temperaments. But it must be carefully developed by teaching and analysis, for too much emphasis can never be bestowed upon giving every note in music its proper value, apart from any other rhythmical consideration. For rhythm in piano-playing is so essential a factor in obtaining a good tone-production, that it is imperative to cultivate it with great attention to correctness of outline.

Lack of rhythm, or faulty rhythm, will take all character from a musical performance, and will leave an impression of insipidity and monotony where there is no rhythm, and of irritation where the rhythm is inexact, as the case may be.

Close on the heels of bad rhythm comes the weakness of *always using the same kind of tone* while performing. Plenty of variation of tone-colour is absolutely necessary for inspired and interesting playing on the piano, as, indeed, on all instruments.

On the piano this is more difficult to arrive at than on the stringed or even the wind instruments, and needs much study of the technique of touch. For frequently we cannot understand, after coming out from a concert, why what we appreciated as a really fine performance of a musical work had not arrested our attention more, or aroused keener pleasure. A certain sense of monotony or dullness had crept over us while listening.

Such a feeling, or rather want of feeling, is almost always the result of the performer's failure to grasp the possibilities of his instrument in relation to tone-colour. Everything he plays is in a similar hue of tone, therefore a sameness and lack of life and contrast pervades the whole. It is a strange anomaly that the more beautiful is the touch of the pianist by natural instinct, the more he is apt to fall into the fault of using it indiscriminately in the same strength, because he takes so much personal pride and pleasure in it. It is like the case of singers who are gifted with wonderful top notes, and, therefore, are always inclined to warble them forth in full but monotonous volumes of sound.

OTHER SERIOUS FAULTS

There are other serious faults which hamper pianists, pertaining more to purely technical matters. Such is, for instance, *sticking out the thumb,* instead of always keeping it ready underneath the palm of the hand in order to facilitate its rapid passage during the changes of position on the keyboard. This is an important affair, as if this sticking out of the thumb is not checked, it will impede the technical perfection of passage-playing and cause it to be awkward, heavy and laboured.

Keeping the elbows out is a trick that many fall into, which is both unsightly and detrimental to tone-production, because it forces the hand into unnatural positions, and stiffens the wrists, as well as impairs rapidity and suppleness of execution.

Excessive movement of the body, too, while playing, is disturbing to the sight and to the player's power of elasticity, yet it is a bad habit which is much indulged in. No doubt it seems to help people to intensify what they are feeling, but this is an illusion. Exaggerated gesture, on the contrary, tends rather to diminish an impression which might otherwise be deep, and weakens it, by a suggestion of hysteria, while too frequently it borders on the ridiculous, in which case the impression is altogether lost. Movements of the body while playing can be divided into two classes, namely, jerky movements (generally confined to the head and shoulders), which produce stiffness and tension, and swaying movements of the whole frame, which disturb the rhythm.

DON'T MAKE FACES

Some players pick up the peculiarity of *making extraordinary faces* during their performance of music. This is a very absurd fault, but it too often becomes a habit that is terribly hard to get rid of, because it is done quite unconsciously as a rule, and is also instigated by a desire to express the maximum of emotion, and sometimes provoked by the physical exertion necessary for the performance of a technical feat. The only remedy for " making faces " is to have a mirror hung in front of the culprit whenever he is practising.

And how about the student who loves his right hand better than his left? He seems to follow the Bible maxim of not letting his right hand know what his left hand is doing, chiefly because his left hand is not doing much at all! By this I mean that it is bad to *neglect the left hand,* which is generally the weaker member, anyhow, and not to allow it to develop its fundamental notes with just as much significance and sonority as the more obvious work of the right hand. Of course, the left hand should never be permitted to drown the right hand, but it should sustain and harmoniously support it.

Young players also err very often by *incorrect style* in their performance of different kinds of music. Bach cannot be played with the highly-coloured romantic passion which should pervade renderings of Schumann or Tschaikovsky, nor with the weird ethereal atmosphere that surrounds the music of the modern French school. Music approached thus in a totally false appreciation of its spirit becomes merely caricature. Yet I have had Chopin played to me with all the dryness and precision of the most pedantic classical manner, and Bach distorted with *rubato* and unnatural limelight effects.

It is perhaps disheartening to think that there are so many pitfalls lurking for the pianist in every direction, but there remains always this consoling reflection, that the man of real genius, even when he suffers from every one of the faults mentioned here, will' not thereby be prevented from still being a great player. These deficiencies of detail are only grave hindrances to the commonplace ability which has no divine fire to sustain it. And when all is said and done, each individual possesses the right to hope that the spark of genius which palliates so many evils may lie in him too, if only it can be discovered.

I well remember Leschetitzky, the greatest of pianoforte teachers, finishing up his lessons to his dejected pupils, after telling them in his most forceful manner of all their heinous faults, with the following exhortation: " I would say nothing, gentlemen, of the manner in which you play, if only the result was a satisfying one. You may play with your feet upon the keyboard if only it sounds well, but remember they must be talented feet."

CHAPTER X

HOW TO PLAY WITH EXPRESSION AND HOW TO USE THE PEDAL

THE true interpretative artist should not only be content with "letting the music speak for itself" (to borrow a stereotyped phrase of those critics who regard personal thought and individuality as a source of reproach). Such a passive attitude is merely looking at the musical art from the standpoint of photography. No; rather must the interpreter endeavour to step into the composer's shoes, to imagine with the poignancy of his imagination, to feel again what he felt, and by so doing to rekindle in the music all the power of fantasy, life and individuality with which it was originally endowed by its creator.

For music is essentially an art that demands interpretation—at least, for its highest effect and appeal. There are continual controversies about this aspect of music, but in my opinion the pianist whose part it is to be the public performer must find in the interpretation of the music the kernel of his whole profession.

Of course, the boundary line between interpretation and the odious vices of distortion and perversion must be kept carefully in view, and for this reason there are some basic rules to guide the student, from which it is impossible to diverge, and it is about some of these that I wish to speak here.

As regards what is now commonly called classical music, as distinct from the romantic or modern creations, it comprises most of the compositions that were written up till the death of Beethoven in 1826. In this kind of music the ideas and effects are for the most part presented by means of certain recognized and distinct forms of expression, and these, though greatly amplified and varied according to the genius of the composer, remain very similar as regards the main structural features.

Around this great school of musical thought, which contains some of the finest treasures of pianoforte literature, many traditions have arisen as to the methods by which the interpretation of such masterpieces should be approached. This is due partly to the distance that separates us from the time of their creation, but mainly to the fact that some pre-eminently great performers have given renderings of these works at various periods, which renderings have been handed down by their pupils and followers, who afterwards themselves became teachers on a lesser plane. Thus the tradition grew up from teacher to student, until by degrees it crystallized itself into a prescribed and definite point of view that has to be taken into account.

NEW LIGHTS ON TRADITION

It is to-day, as always, the mission of the authoritative interpreter to amplify and throw new lights upon these traditions, and not be content to accept the general version which his less-gifted brethren have to subscribe to with reverent faith. Still, even for the great artist the fundamental principles must remain the same, and for him, as for the student, they will form the guiding line of his mental vision.

Of course, I know that there is a school of musical thought which practically condemns any effort at interpretation or emotion in music. They like to be given just the notes as they were written down, like so many words recited without a shadow of life or expression. Artists have often been much called to task by critics who hold such views because their interpretations of the masterpieces of music are based on the natural conviction that the greater the music, the more power of colour, fine feeling and poetry it ought to be able to express. It is difficult to understand the people who talk with arrogant authority about how exactly a musical work should be interpreted. They like to invest it with a sort of traditional dryness of expression which tends to render especially the older of the great classics a sort of trial of tediousness which many genuine music lovers submit to endure only as a kind of educational duty. It is, I am sure, a good deal a matter of temperament that controls these radical divergences of ideas about musical performance. It seems to me that to hold such views is not to get any further than mere arrangements of detail and narrow perspective, while the true majesty of the picture is missed. I have many times met truly musical people who found Bach and Beethoven dull, and were surprised at having been stirred by a great fugue or sonata which they had never appreciated before. And I am certain it was because they had never been allowed the opportunity of realizing the full glory of such music. For can one imagine a nobler or wider range in which to find every wealth of imagination, intellect and feeling than is to be found in the great sonatas of Beethoven.

The earliest pianoforte music we know of was written in the form of simple dance measures such as courantes, allemandes, pavanes, gigues and so forth. These were performed upon very primitive-keyed instruments, amongst the best known being the virginals, harpischords and spinets, and they were only suitable to the plainest methods of treatment.

Indeed, the story is told of Dr. Arne, the celebrated eighteenth-century English composer, that he said about one of those instruments, " It is the devil's own instrument, my masters, like the scratch of a quill with a squeak at the end of it."

Only since the variety and capacity of instruments have developed, and also since Bach created the complex and polyphonic harmonies which revolutionized pianoforte music, has the scope of harmonical expression become so greatly enlarged, and the problems which surround it so complicated. The discovery of the pedal, too, changed the whole complexion of interpretation on the piano, while in the light of modern technique it seems strange to think that before the advent of Bach the use of the thumb and also of the 5th finger was absolutely forbidden by the best teachers.

In those days the wrist was held high and the hand stiff; a high chair was no doubt also used for sitting at the instrument, and the whole attitude while playing must have been one of rigidity and precision. Any rendering of this primitive music was necessarily very quiet and limited in the means employed. All violent *crescendo* or *diminuendo* effects were impossible, and the rhythm was confined to the swaying but monotonous lilt of the gigues of that day, or to the more stately measures of the pavanes. Certainly it would seem, to say the least of it, indecorous to play a piece of the sixteenth century even on a modern pianoforte with the abandonment of a Liszt Rhapsody, or, vice versa, to render the passionate music of Chopin or Liszt with the demure coldness of the early masters. This is where a sense of style should come in, to help the artist in his conception of the different aspects of musical composition.

MUSICAL STYLE

And what is musical style? I think it can be explained as the impression reflected upon the music by the manners, customs, and modes of thought which were characteristic of the epoch when it was written. For, after all, people lived, loved and suffered every kind of emotion in former centuries just as we do now, only each period has had its diverse ways of expressing these things in the arts.

What, then, do we mean by the interpretation of music itself for the purpose of performance? Is it not the employing of all possible technical means to infuse the spirit of life into the inanimate musical form, and cause it to be kindled into a definite sound-picture for the mind of the listener? On the pianoforte this is done by means of accents, variations of tone-values (*crescendo* and *diminuendo*), variations of rhythm (*accellerando* and *ritardando*), variety of touch, and manipulation of the pedals. Accents enable the pianist to bring into prominence certain notes, or groups of notes, which might be comparable to cries, exclamations, interjections in the elocutionary art, or to sudden bursts of colour in painting.

These and other similes could be followed up through the whole scale of human emotions, for the well-trained hand of the pianist, being the pliant tool of his imagination, represents to him what the brush does to the painter, or the voice to the actor. And many of the same æsthetic laws govern all these in their work as far as is possible, when the difference of circumstance and material is taken into account.

RULES OF INTERPRETATION

As far as the general rules of interpretation are concerned, I will give a few which appertain to what might be called the syntax of music. Such are the following. An ascending passage should be played with a *crescendo,* a descending passage with a *diminuendo.* The pedal must be changed according to the harmonies, in order to blend the tones, and to enable notes to be held on which the fingers could not manage without its assistance. Rhythm, too, as distinct from time, must be clearly marked, so as to indicate where accents ought to fall, and to create atmosphere. Music played without true rhythm will always sound colourless and insipid. Time should also be well defined, that it may preserve the general form of the composition.

Skilful use of all these means makes up the art of interpreting, and it is for the mentality of the pianist to employ them in their varying degrees, to mould them, combine them, and dispose of them, and thus invest the whole work with the pulsating breath of actuality. No doubt there must exist in the interpreter a natural good taste which will govern his outlook, and this can only spring from a sound musical instinct trained by education, and by hearing great artists perform. For it goes without saying that there are no absolute rules about interpretation. There can but be some broad outlines of style and taste to stimulate the imagination of the student, and help him in his task.

As I have already pointed out, the interpretations of the masterpieces of music by great artists become established as traditions. Still the personal thought of the performer should make its influence felt in the rendering of all music, even of the most classical type, if that rendering is to be of any real value and interest, only this personality has to conform to the general dicta of the style. Thus it will be found that no two fine artists will interpret a piece in the same way. There may be a thousand

FIG. 31. Opening subject of Chopin's Prelude in F major.

1.—Medium *Tempo*. Accompaniment very *legato* in the right hand and fingers very near the keyboard. No *crescendo* or *diminuendo*. The impression is one of complete tranquillity or twilight.

differences of expression in their particular performance, and each of them equally correct. This fact only illustrates how imagination and colour may be infused into interpretation in much variety. For great musical compositions may well be compared to beautiful landscapes, which are ever-changing in colour and effect through the action of atmospheric conditions. On no two days does the country look alike, yet its composition and outline remain fixed, everlasting.

It is told of Beethoven that he played over one of his own compositions to a talented pupil in order to give him some idea of the interpretative side, and then asked the student to play the same piece again. This was done, and the master complimented him, remarking that although it differed greatly from the original, it was decidedly better.

This reminds me of Tchaikovsky, who was asked, after conducting a composition of his own, why he did not do so in the same way as he had once done before. "My friend," the master replied, "if you ever see me conduct this again, it will be different still. It is merely a matter of mood."

To show how different renderings of the same piece may be possible without the structure of the work being in any way altered, I give on page 80 two interpretations of the opening subject of Chopin's Prelude in F Major, which both possess equal merit. (See Figs. 31 and 32.)

Fig. 32. Another rendering of the same subject.

2.—Slow *Tempo*. Accompaniment in the right hand half-strength with thrown fingers—left-hand melody brought out with accents as marked. In the right hand undulating movement expressed by a *diminuendo* and *crescendo*. The impression is one of movement—birds singing, or water rippling.

Another detail which it is necessary for the student to bear in mind is that technical passages ought never to be played as if they were of purely digital dexterity, as this method makes of such passages only hard, uninteresting interludes of display, wearisome to the listener and of no value musically. All technical passages, even the most difficult ones, should be considered as embroideries of the main harmonies; in fact, they are the rhetoric of the composition.

Melody also should *not* be knocked out with unbalanced enthusiasm to the entire detriment of the accompaniment, nor should any two notes of a melody be given with exactly the same tone-colour, for this will create monotony of sound. Every single tone should be on a general scale of gradation, each having its own place in the scheme of chiaroscuro; because the mechanical tone of the piano itself, with which we are dealing, makes it imperative that every device to conjure up perspective and charm should be brought into service, and above all typewriting effects of precise striking must be strenuously avoided.

THE ATTITUDE OF THE HANDS

In fact, the keyboard ought never to be struck hard at all in *legato* passages or in melody of any kind. On the contrary, the keys must be caressed with a sort of almost stroking movement, to obtain the requisite tone-values. And in connection with this there is another thing to which I attach great importance, namely, that the hand in its attitude on the keyboard should reflect in some degree the spirit of the music.

For instance, it would not be natural to hold the hands as formally when playing Chopin as in the performance of sixteenth-century music. Again, in a vivacious piece the hands should look sprightly and full of energy, while in slow cantabile movements they should present a soft and sinuous appearance. For even the fact of the hand looking hard and stiff during playing will assuredly affect the sound adversely, and rob it of beauty of quality.

All these things are intimately connected with the preparation of a fine touch upon the piano. The word " touch," as a musical term, signifies really the mode by which the fingers attack the keyboard. For the great difficulty to be contended with on the piano when it is necessary to produce a singing tone lies in this, that by its mechanical composition, if once a key is struck upon the instrument, no further modification of the sound-quality is possible. No *vibrato* or mellowing of the tone can be afterwards applied as on stringed instruments; with the piano, all is over when the finger has once fallen and the hammer has struck the strings.

Therefore anything that can be done to sweeten the tone must be attempted before the striking of the note. By this I mean that an *infinitesimal* time should elapse between the action of lifting the finger to strike and the definite falling of the finger upon the key. Touch must be thus prepared in the playing of all melody and singing passages with a slow pressing movement of the hand and fingers. This caressing touch could not, of course, be employed in rapid difficult passages, where direct quick blows of the fingers are indispensable in order to save time. In such cases, and in the higher development of technical brilliance, no more lifting of the fingers is necessary than is compatible with distinct articulation.

" THE SOUL OF THE PIANO "

I now come to the loud or sustaining pedal, which Rubinstein aptly called " the soul of the piano." It certainly is the best friend the pianist has at his disposal for helping him to overcome the material drawbacks of the pianoforte's constitution, and without it no *legato* playing or prolongation of tone would be possible at all.

Of course, there are two pedals on the modern pianoforte, even sometimes three, but the soft one is only used, as its name implies, for deadening the sound. The loud pedal, as it is called, is the real important factor, and when I speak of the pedal in future as a general term, it is always to this one that I am referring. The name "loud pedal" is really a misnomer, as its function is rather to sweeten the sound and render it more open, and also to add brilliance to the tone rather than actual loudness. If the pedal is a good friend it can also be the worst possible enemy if badly employed. Nothing is more terrible than the general blur cast over everything by the pedal when it is applied without expert knowledge. A few simple rules about how it should be used are as follows.

I have already mentioned that the pedal must be changed on different harmonies; it should also never be taken directly on the first beat of the bar to obtain the best results, but in syncopation with that beat, as in the example below.

DO NOT IMPAIR DISTINCTNESS

The pedal can also be used in passages to give a more sustaining quality to the tone, though here care must be taken not to impair distinctness, but a great deal more pedal can be applied without causing any blur if an accent is given on the bass note on which the passage is built. The pedal may be applied in a greater degree in the higher than in the lower registers of the instrument, as the higher tones can stand, and also need, more sustaining than the lower ones, whilst these last possess of themselves a certain sustenance of tone, and therefore blur more quickly. When applying the pedal it should never be banged on, but pressed down gently and gradually.

It is essential to possess a good knowledge of harmony in order to be able to apply the pedal correctly, for it is necessary when using it to understand something about the structure of chords. All blurring over of tone by the pedal produces a most unpleasant impression upon the ear, and must be rigorously guarded against, except when, in some particular passage, a special effect is required, such as in the F minor Ballade of Chopin, in the example given below.

But this is only an outlying instance which really appertains to the most elaborate study of tone-colour.   The general elementary

FIG. 33. Prelude in D flat (Chopin).
Example showing the pedal taken in syncopation with the beat.

It will be noticed that the pedal is taken directly after the note is struck and not
on it, the finger not being released until the pedal is pressed down.   The clamp
under the bass part indicates the exact duration of holding down the pedal.

rule for the student, however, remains that the blurring of tones by the pedal is bad—in fact, it is one of the worst faults a pianist can commit.   Professional pianists use the pedal very much more than amateurs, but it will not be so apparent in their playing.   This is because the experienced artist takes his pedal in a correct way

FIG. 34. Example showing special blurring effect of pedal in Chopin's
F minor Ballade.

Here the pedal is taken for two bars instead of being changed at each bar.   This
is done to obtain an effect of surging water, or the wind whistling through the
trees.   The clamp under the bass part indicates the exact duration of holding
down the pedal.

harmonically, so that it blends the tones naturally and does not upset the outlines, while the player who does not possess the understanding or the training neglects to change the pedal with the harmonies, and thereby produces a smudge of sound instead of clear colour.

The pedal is indeed the essence of life to the pianoforte, and by managing it wisely the pianist will conjure up out of his music the most vivid and satisfying impressions, while to the lovers of beautiful sound there can be no more fascinating study than the many and varied combinations which the pedal is able to obtain by the binding together of different tone-colours.

CHAPTER XI

HOW TO MAKE THE PIANO SING

WHAT is the most elusive and difficult thing to teach, and yet at the same time the most necessary of all the powers which a pianist must acquire to be successful in his art? Is it not surely the power to produce a fine, noble singing tone from his instrument?

The study of tone on the pianoforte in all its infinite varieties of loudness and softness, of roundness, of purity, of abruptness, or sensuousness, is as intricate and absorbing as anything in the world of musical technique. For it combines within itself not only the highest technical attainment, but also much that properly belongs to the province of interpretation and inspiration.

Looking at the piano merely from the standpoint of a mechanical instrument, it is wonderful to realize how much can be done by the skill and taste of the player to vary and qualify the sound it gives out. Constantly people are heard to say, "How he makes the instrument sing!" This is the kernel of the whole matter, namely, to "make the instrument sing." It is not enough to play clearly, to play fast, to play slowly, to play loudly, to play softly; all these different gradations must be alive with the requisite tone to make them real and atmospheric.

THE STUDY OF TONE

Tone represents to the pianist what colour does to the painter, and some artists possess a finer perception of that quality than others. Besides, some pianists are not mainly interested in the study of tone, but are content with striking the keys always more or less in the same way, either loud or soft, or *mezzoforte,* as the case may be. In the performance of the more modern and romantic schools of musical compositions such as Chopin and Schumann, and those of our own day, this indifference to variety of tone will pass muster more or less easily, as this kind of music is in itself generally so full of colour and elaborate harmony in its combinations of sound that the lack of much subtlety of tone on the player's part will not be so much felt. And this more especially upon the modern pianoforte, which yields a good full tone without any effort if not struck too directly.

But when playing classical music a dry or prosaic tone is a terrible drawback, for it renders it, even to musical people, tedious and wearying to listen to, because of the dead monotonous delivery of the performer. Whereas if each chord, each phrase, each melody is reverently thought out and made to glow with beauty and variety of tone, all the glory and worth of the great music can be brought home to those very listeners who otherwise might have been bored by it.

Beauty, and with it variety, of tone, can be obtained on the pianoforte by several means. Rhythm has something to do with it. Pressure of the fingers when striking the notes affects it; suppleness and elasticity of the wrists help to attain it. In melody, tone should be caressed out of the piano, melting one note into another by an undulating movement of the hand. In sparkling technical passages it should be outlined concisely by means of rhythm, in the way of accents in some places, and in others by careful divisions of values, with regard to the balance of light and shade in the structure of the passage. Such conciseness of tone will produce a fine relief for the technical ornamentations and impart to them vigour and brilliance.

AVOID HARSHNESS

Great power of tone is very difficult to produce without harshness, for chords struck with direct and powerful blows of the hand will emit hard, metallic sounds that must shock the ear. But if the strength is concentrated and applied through the forearm to the keys, the fingers being pressed down into the notes as if about to force a great weight out of the piano, the harshness will be avoided, and a full, deep singing tone will be the result.

Sometimes in a concerto with the orchestra the piano is left alone suddenly to usher in a grand and powerful phrase, the orchestra having just before been playing with immense tone and wealth of sound. This happens, for instance, at the end of the last movement of Grieg's Pianoforte Concerto. (See Fig. 35.) In such a place, unless the pianist can bring his tone up to something approximating to the volume and richness which the orchestra has just left off giving out, the phrase which he now has to bring in alone will miss its whole effect. His performance of it will give the impression of a poor, stilted, hard imitation of the orchestra, or, in fact, it will sound like the effort of a mouse trying to carry

on the work of a lion.   So to accomplish this tremendous balance
of tone with a whole orchestra against him the pianist must be
able to combine great strength with depth and sonority.

The grandiose cadenza of chords in the opening bars of Liszt's
Pianoforte Concerto in E flat is another instance where hardness
of tone makes the whole passage unbearable, instead of, as it should
be, if given with the right quality of sound, profound, and fraught
with an atmosphere of impending excitement.   (See Fig. 23, page
57.)

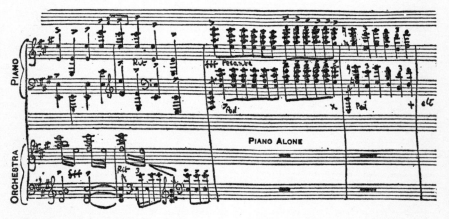

Fig. 35. The end of the last movement of Grieg's Pianoforte Concerto in
A minor, showing after two bars that piano is left alone to continue in
triple forte.

For if a pianist just comes down like a sledge-hammer upon
the chords, as some do when endeavouring to obtain great power
of tone, it only degenerates into mere noise, and can contain none
of the epic quality with which a grand sequence of *fortissimo* chords
should be invested.   In *pianissimo* tone much the same sort of thing
applies as regards the quality of it.   If the tone produced is only a
quiet sound, the result of a very gentle fall of the finger on the
key and nothing more, what is there in it?   It may be soft, but
it will remain cold, impersonal, insipid, without any æsthetic value
or significance.   Therefore the pianist's business is to put warmth
and tenderness into the softness, so that, though *pianissimo,* the
sound clings and appeals to the ear.

Abrupt chords and outstanding notes at the end of a passage
are also difficult to play with sufficient terseness without sacrificing
beauty of tone; but here again concentration of the force of the
blow given will rob it of the hard noise of the impact, without
losing one jot of its energetic character.

One of the best developments of tone-production on the piano is to be able to strike the same note several times, and each time not only to make a *crescendo* or a *diminuendo* of the sound, but also to give an actual change in the character of the tone. In a *decrescendo* where the repeated note has to die away, it is most essential to get this change of tone quality, as it is so true to nature. Every time a natural echo resounds again the tone loses a little more of its significance and the quality diminishes, and thus, too, must it be managed on the piano.

It is a good deal owing to clever manipulation of the pedal that such an effect can be produced, and also to a constant modification of the mode of attacking the note. Upon each occasion that the hand strikes the note it should approach closer and closer to the key, until at last the action becomes the merest pressure of the finger on the note to bring forth the final vague tone, that floats into nothing at the end of the echo.

BAD INSTRUMENTS

The pianist who has attained a perfect development of tone-quality ought to be able to make a melody sound well on any piano, even the old cracked tin-kettle sort of variety one sometimes finds in country villages. This will be no partly due to his high technical skill, but also because the artist who makes a great study of tone-colour comes to obtain a sort of intuition, after he has played on any instrument for a few moments, as to how he can obtain the best results from it, even when the means at his disposal are very limited.

Therefore it is not always a disadvantage to the student to have only an indifferent instrument to practise on at home, for he is obliged to take far more pains to arrive at a fine tone-production on his poor piano. He will consequently learn more at the outset of the particular technique necessary for its achievement, and will possess a wider range of experience to apply when he reaches the possibility of more adequate means of expression.

The pedal, of course, is the greatest adjunct the pianist possesses to sweeten and enrich his tone, though it may equally well ruin its quality unless applied with much care and technical understanding. For if the pedal is carelessly used, and blurs and slurs over everything, nothing comes of it save a heavy atmosphere of unclean tone.

This fault is almost worse than harshness or monotony. And

it is monotonous in any case, just as much as tone that is unsweet-
ened by the pedal, because the continual blur of this murky sound
wearies the ear almost .beyond endurance. But intelligent study
of the effects of the pedal, and careful management in changing
it when the basic harmonies of the music alter, can develop it
into the most precious essential for imparting warmth and life
to tone.

Still, an initial dry and hard tone-production on the player's
part cannot be entirely transformed or beautified by application of
the pedal, however skilfully it is done. This is because the pianist's
finger-attack is at the outset hard and direct in the actual striking of
the keys, instead of being caressing, and there is nothing to be
done until this fault is eradicated. So when practising it is a good
thing to endeavour to produce a melting and sustained tone in
melody without first applying the pedal at all; and the same should
be done with chords.

The pianist should learn to attack them with power and volume
of sound, avoiding harsh blows, before evoking the pedal to come
to his help. Then, when he is able to produce beauty of tone-
quality unaided, he can study pedal effects with profit and enhance-
ment to his playing.

A PIANIST'S BEST INSPIRATION

Some people no doubt are endowed with a natural facility for
producing a beautiful tone on the piano, generally owing to the
particular constructions of their hands, which are pliable, elastic
and sinuous by nature. But I think that, with sufficient careful
study and attention given to the subject, every player can arrive at
its acquirement, even though to some it seems a greater difficulty
than to others.

Anyhow, it is one of the most necessary branches of pianoforte
technique, and without possessing it the pianist will find it impossible to make charm or poetry of expression emanate from his
instrument.

I can think of no more fitting conclusion to a chapter on beauty
of tone than to refer to Anton Rubinstein's attitude towards this
question. For that master of touch, who was undoubtedly one of
the greatest exponents of " how to sing on the piano," used always
to tell his pupils that he had acquired his knowledge from listening
to the singing of the great tenor Rubini. He happened to hear
Rubini sing one day, and was so impressed by the wonderful

quality of his sound-production that ever afterwards his ideal remained to reproduce something of the tone of Rubini's voice upon his piano. Certainly, Rubinstein's idea that the sound of a beautiful human voice is the best inspiration for the pianist to imbibe is one which every student of tone-production would do well to follow.

Chapter XII

A SPECIMEN LESSON: THE "MOONLIGHT SONATA"
FIRST MOVEMENT (BEETHOVEN)

I HAVE chosen the first movement of the Sonata in C sharp minor of Beethoven, commonly known as the "Moonlight Sonata," as the subject of my specimen lesson, because it is so universally beloved by all sorts and conditions of people, and is so well known. It is, therefore, one which all students of the pianoforte must learn. I will first give a short history of the Sonata, as this should also be of special interest to students.

The Sonata in C sharp minor, which was entitled by Beethoven himself "Quasi una Fantasia," was one of two sonatas written in the year 1801 and published in March, 1802, and forming together Opus 27. These years of 1801 and 1802 were of great creative activity on the part of Beethoven, and his works produced during this time belong to what is general classified as the Master's second period.

Grove says that the Sonata in C sharp minor was dedicated to the Contessa Gulietta Guicciardi, and much romance has been invented on this score. But the lady herself rather discounts this romance by recounting how Beethoven gave her the Rondo in G, and then, wanting to dedicate something to the Princess Lichnowsky, he took the Rondo away and gave the Contessa the "Moonlight Sonata" in its place. In my own edition of the Sonata, which is an old one published by Hallberger in Stuttgart in 1858, and edited by Moscheles, the pianist, a personal friend of Beethoven, it is stated to be dedicated to the Princess of Liechtenstein.

The title "The Moonlight," was supposed to have been given to the Sonata by Rellstab, a celebrated contemporary musical critic, who compared the first movement to a moonlight scene on the Lake of Lucerne. But it may also have received the name from a publisher who, after the custom of publishers, christened several of Beethoven's sonatas by various titles in order to make them more popular with the public (such as the "Pathétique," "Pastorale," "Les Adieux, L'Absence, Le Retour," etc.). I myself think the title of "Moonlight" not inappropriate to the spirit of the first movement of the C sharp minor Sonata, which reflects the romantic atmosphere and mysterious light and shade connected with the presence of the moon. But certainly the last movement has nothing to do with moonlight, but represents a great storm of emotion, where all is cloud, wind and fury.

WHY IT IS POPULAR

The Sonata in C sharp minor was a great favourite from the moment of its publication, and Beethoven jokingly even pretended to be annoyed about it, as he considered many of his other sonatas to be finer works musically; but still the " Moonlight Sonata " remains a warm favourite. Probably the fact, technically, the lovely slow movement with which it commences is well within the reach of very moderate performers on the pianoforte may help to account for its extreme popularity over its fellows, since so many amateurs are able to derive pleasure from their own rendering of it.

Beethoven wrote thirty-two sonatas in all, of which certainly nearly half are still as beloved and admired as ever they were, and continue to form an absolutely essential part of the repertoire of every pianist. He brought the sonata form to its highest perfection, and, having found the models of his predecessors too stilted and formal for the wider expression of his thoughts, he made innovations of what in those days were considered the most daring kind, and improved upon the forms he found. Like all original men of genius, he could not tolerate being fettered by conventions, and his mighty spirit soared untrammelled.

The " Moonlight Sonata " is one of Beethoven's most original compositions of the so-called second period of his works, and in it he shows his freedom of thought by commencing the Sonata with an *adagio* movement which is not in sonata form, and which was at the time an entire innovation. In fact, the whole work is a precursor of the modern sonata. According to Beethoven's own directions the three movements were to be played straight through to the end without a break. He puts " Attacca subito il sequente " after each movement, showing that the three movements were designed to represent a continuous thread of thought running throughout the whole work. This unusual and free treatment of the Sonata's structure has imparted to it a modernity and freshness which ensure it an everlasting place in the literature of the pianoforte.

THE FIRST MOVEMENT

The first movement of the " Moonlight Sonata " consists of a haunting and beautiful melody, full of romance and pathos,

floating on a continuous stream of undulating harmony. The
interpretation of it should be of the highest imagination, glowing
with a quiet radiance of fantasy and feeling. The tone employed
must be warm and melting in quality, imparting at the same time
the mysterious resignation and the vague unrest of the music's
atmosphere. The opening five bars should be played in a manner
to convey a kind of rhythmical stream to the triplet figures, and
thus create an impression as of a continuously undulating back-

Example No. 1, bars 1-4.

ground for the melody which is presently to start. The octaves
in the bass should be played somewhat louder than the triplet
figure in the right hand, so as to produce the requisite depth of
tone, though the volume of sound should not overstep the bounds
of "piano" (*p*).—*Ex. No. 1, bars 1-4.*

Example No. 2, bar 10.

The melody is introduced in the
fifth bar, and must give the idea
of floating on the accompaniment.
At the tenth bar there comes a
change of harmony from the
major into the minor key, and
here the note G (the first G) in
the right hand should be accentuated.—*Ex. No. 2, bar 10.*

Proceeding onwards to the last quarter of the fifteenth bar and
leading to the sixteenth, the melody adopts a more insistent temper,
which may be rendered by emphasizing the notes B and C of the
melody in the right hand, especially the C. In fact, this note C

should be taken arpeggiato with the accompaniment underneath. It seems to me to represent a cry of unutterable heart-ache, a sudden longing which cannot be appeased. In the following bar, where these same notes of appeal appear again, they may be repeated *pianissimo* as a kind of echo.—*Ex. No. 3, bars* 15-18.

Example No. 3, bars 15–18.

Coming to the twenty-fifth bar, there seems to be like a second voice appearing with a question in the treble and an answer in the base, and then another question, and the answer. In these bars the amount of tone can be somewhat increased and a plaintive expression imparted to the questioning phrases.—*Ex. No. 4, bars* 28-31.

Example No. 4, bars 28-31.

A similar development is to be found in bars thirty and thirty-one. At bar thirty-two a storm begins to rise in the harmonies,

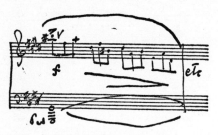

and continues to increase with a gradually ascending *crescendo* of tone and *accellerando* of movement until it reaches its culminating point on the first note (B sharp) of the thirty-sixth bar, which should be brought out with considerable force.—*Ex. No. 5, bar* 36.

Example No. 5, bar 36.

From here onward the storm of emotion gradually diminishes in intensity until it returns with a *rallentando* in the fortieth and forty-first bars to the subdued spirit of the original atmosphere of the piece. It is of great importance during the gradual calming down of the stress of the music from bars thirty-seven to forty, that the melody which has embodied itself in the inner structures of the harmonies should be brought out thus. —*Ex. No. 6, bars* 37-40.

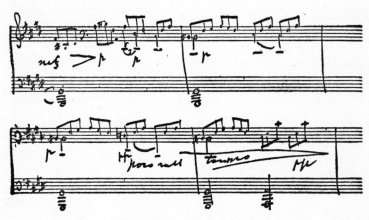

Example No. 6, bars 37-40.

The next part of the movement resumes the opening melody, and then continues its course with some variation on the original, both in modulation of key and progression of passages. In the fifty-sixth and fifty-seventh bars the melody should be especially brought out and made apparent above the rhythmical figures of the accompaniment.—*Ex. No. 7, bars* 56-57.

The movement now sinks towards its close, and from the sixtieth to the sixty-fourth bar the fateful notes in the left hand right down

Example No. 7, bars 56-57.

in the bass must resound, though not louder than *mezzo-forte,* but still with an ominous emphasis which should pervade the last few bars of the movement.—*Ex. No. 8, bars* 60-63.

Example No. 8, bars 60-63.

Again, from bars sixty-four to sixty-eight, these deep bass notes should speak out like the ringing of a knell of doom, but this time, though equally distinct as before, they should be given as soft as possible, like an echo of the former ones. The movement is thus brought to a conclusion in an atmosphere of melancholy tinged with vague foreboding.

Chapter XIII

PLAYING IN PUBLIC

It is an art almost to be acquired of itself to play in public with success, that is to say, to interest and give pleasure to the audience, and at the same time to afford more or less satisfaction to the performer's sense of achievement. For, no matter how good a training has been gone through, or how much technical means has been mastered, none of this seems to count for much in the naked and exposed atmosphere of the public platform. For there Magnetism, Personality and Power of Concentration, are the only sources of communication by which the pianist may hope to convince his hearers.

And in order to stimulate in his performances these three great essentials, it is imperative for him to throw himself so completely into his work while on the platform as to become oblivious of his surroundings, and thus be transformed into a complete medium, or vehicle of transmission, between the composer's ideas and the audience. I am persuaded that at certain moments during a performance the magnetism of the player compelling the attention of his listeners, creates in him a sort of state of hypnotism. Hence I have often noticed the fact, that any sudden outside noise in the hall, however slight, will startle the performer almost out of his wits, and give him a shock quite out of proportion to its small significance, and this because his mind was not at the moment quite sentient of its actuality.

A SPECIAL GIFT

There is no doubt that some people have a special gift, or are temperamentally predisposed for appearing in public; the throbbing expectancy of the crowd around them acts as a stimulus to the activity of their brains and imagination. To the student who has such a temperament (and most of those who succeed in becoming great interpretative artists possess it), there is only a question of time and experience before he learns to feel instinctively the varying moods of his audiences. Once having acquired this sensitiveness to receive impressions from his public, it will be his privilege to compel them to follow him in all he does, and thus an understanding between them will be soon perfectly established.   And when this understanding is accomplished, I have found that the performer ceases to be conscious of his surroundings any more, because all adverse elements have become reconciled and he can lose himself in his interpretation, secure that the mind of the public is with him.   But as long as the artist is conscious of their presence through unquietness amongst them, coughs, whispers and restlessness, etc., so long is his spell not woven.   Then will he put all the resources of his technical equipment into play to endeavour to produce the magnetic current from himself to the audience.

Possibly it may be a monotony of tone which prevents him reaching them; to counteract this he will try to change and vary his tone-colour with greater subtlety, or he may feel that the rhythm is not charged with life. He will then strive to put more pulsation into it in order to focus the attention of the public and to give a finer relief to the music he is setting before them, so that their minds cannot fail to apprehend its beauty.   For though many single individuals in an audience may know nothing and care little for music, yet the general collective mass of a great big public can be galvanized into becoming like one single vibrating nerve, responding instantaneously to every variation of colour, rhythm and passion.

" ABSOLUTE MUSICIANS "

Now all good musicians who play instruments are what I call absolute musicians, that is to say, they depend entirely and solely on the music for their expression of thought.   They are independent of all gesture, word or scenery, and their appeal is a direct one to the emotions, through the medium of combinations of sound, variously presented.   Therefore has music in the widest sense no bounds of nationality, no stumbling blocks of race or language to confine it.   Its appeal can be felt as well in Kamschatka or Terra del Fuego as in London and Paris.

I have played the Beethoven "Moonlight" and "Appasssionata" Sonatas alike to gold miners and empire builders in South Africa, to cowboys and millionaires in the Western States of America, to ranchers and railway magnates in Canada, even to Maoris in New Zealand, and Chinamen in Vancouver, and found they all listened and were interested even when they did not quite understand.   And it is a curious fact that I have noted the finest masterpieces of music almost always produce a greater impression than inferior works on audiences which are more or less uneducated musically.

Another strange thing which I have personally experienced is, that sometimes when I am feeling unfit physically, at the crucial moment I will very likely play better than usual. The effort is a greater one for me, but no doubt my mind, having to be more alert to overcome bodily weakness, acts consequently more powerfully all around. I do not mean to say for a moment by this that it is an advantage in public playing to be in a weak state physically; that would obviously be an absurdity. In fact, there is of course no public profession where good, sound bodily health and strength are not necessary essentials to success, because the wear and tear of excitement are so continuous. But the mind, and imagination and temperament controlled by the mind, must always be the dominant factors of every sort of condition and remain undisturbed by unexpected eventualities. And in this dominance over conditions lies what I call the technique of the platform, and comprises also the mastery of such things as different acoustical properties of the place the pianist is called upon to play in. This may often prove a difficult problem and require much experience to negotiate successfully, especially if the artist has only to appear for a short performance and that in a building where he has not played before.

But by long experience the pianist can more or less tell after striking a few preliminary chords the kind of acoustical difficulty which he will have to contend with. If, for instance, a hall has too much resonance for the piano, then the music must be taken at a slower *tempo* and with more emphasis than elsewhere. In places like the Albert Hall, in London, or the Free Trade Hall, in Manchester, this is the case. It is, of course, a good deal also a matter of perspective and atmosphere. For it is quite obvious that a *fine nuance* which would be perfect in a small place might be entirely lost in the Albert Hall; and vice versa, the emphasis and deliberation necessary to give the right outline to a big declamatory phrase in the Free Trade Hall might sound rough and exaggerated in a building of lesser dimensions. Now the business of the true artist and the best amateur is to propagate the finest art wherever they happen to be. For though the popular tune of the moment may have an immediate success, it will not last, neither can it make any abiding impression. But once a great musical work has struck the imagination of even the most superficial mind, it will leave an uneffaceable memory. In fact it is quite astonishing how many people there are who though otherwise quite unmusical, yet will always go to hear and enjoy one particular great work, such as one certain symphony, or opera, or sonata. And this, just because the special work happened once to make some unforgettable impression upon them, so that they really continue to enjoy it without knowing anything more about other music than before.

To return once more to the kind of magnetic spell which should bind performer and audience together, I wish to show how this power of holding the public, as it is sometimes termed, can be turned to advantage if an outside emergency arises, such as may occur occasionally in every walk of life. I well remember in this connection when I was giving a concert once in St. John's, New Brunswick, Canada, that there being no available concert hall, the performance was held in a big public meeting-room on the first floor of the building. The only entrance to the room was by one rather narrow wooden staircase, and the same staircase was the only way out.

The room was crowded so that there was no space to pass in the hall at all, and people were everywhere, even crowding on the platform. In the middle of my first piece all the electric light went out suddenly, leaving the vast crowd plunged in the blackest darkness. They began to get up and grope for an outlet to the one narrow stair, which in the congested state of the room would soon have caused a panic if it had continued. Luckily I was so absorbed in what I was playing that I never actually noticed that the lights had disappeared and I went on playing quite unconsciously (I think it was a fugue of Bach). And when the audience realized the music was proceeding as if nothing had happened, insistent and commanding as is ever the music of Bach, they subsided into their seats and did not attempt to move again till an attendant, after a short time, found a candle, lit it, put it on the piano and eventually succeeded in extemporizing enough light to keep things going.

Another incident of the same kind happened to me once in Sydney Town Hall, in Australia. It is a vast place, and there were about five thousand people in it that night. During the performance a tropical storm broke out and affected the electric dynamo, so that there also all the light went out, and some foolish people shouted "Fire!" I never noticed anything this time either, so engrossed was I in the music I was playing, and I continued as if nothing had occurred. Here again the public hearing the music still going on regained their tranquillity, supposing that there could not be very much wrong if it was not necessary even to cease playing, and they remained listening without panic till light was procured.

Becoming so absorbed in the music has been a peculiarity of mine since earliest childhood, and when only a little boy of nine it nearly cost me my future career, and incidentally gained me a very fine toy steam engine! I was taken by my father to play before one of the Russian Grand Dukes who was interested in music. I was to play a pianoforte concerto with the orchestra which, if the Grand Duke was satisfied with my performance, and thought I had talent, meant my remaining in Moscow to study. In the middle of the concerto there was a cadenza for the piano which I had to play alone, and then at a given point the orchestra joined in again. While performing this cadenza I somehow got so interested in the musical progressions that I forgot what I was doing, and began developing other progressions and wandering into other keys. The orchestra sat aghast, they did not know how to catch me, the conductor looked terribly dismayed, he could not understand what I was at! Suddenly I came to myself, found I was miles away from the original key, and had to modulate back by a series of chords. Without stopping my playing I managed to get into the right music again and gradually arrived at the point where the orchestra were able to pick me up.

The Grand Duke, who was musical, laughed when the performance was over; he had been entertained by this contretemps. At the same time he was so pleased that I had been able to extricate myself from the imbroglio, that he not only complimented my father about me, but asked me what I should like him to give me. The only thing I wanted in the world at that time was a toy steam-engine and I boldly said so, to the amazement of all present. And I got it too, and a beauty it was! I fear no one would give me an engine now if I wandered off into improvisation in the middle of the cadenza of the Tchaikovsky concerto!

CHAPTER XIV

EPILOGUE: THE PIANO AS A HOUSEHOLD FRIEND,
AND HOW TO CHOOSE AND CARE FOR ONE

THE rapid rise of the piano and the enormous growth in its popularity during the last fifty years is the best tribute to its unparalleled powers of bringing even to the humblest homes a little of the divine spirit of music. This universality of the instrument, and its advantage as a real household friend, is due in a great measure to its accessibility to everyone in the elementary stages of playing. It can yield pleasant effect at once without any great amount of labour, and a little gentle strumming on the piano gives a great deal of joy to many who never meet with any higher form of music in their lives.

The wideness of its scope, too, in the combinations of sound, and its adaptability to serve the moods of every sort of occasion, go to make it one of the most wonderful developments which the science of men has evolved for the nurturing of musical life amongst all sorts and conditions of people. The cracked old piano of a village hall rattling out polkas and waltzes in its tin-kettle voice, but providing plenty of spirit and go for the dance; the hymn tunes reverently fingered out on the much-treasured instrument in the remote country homes; the hospital or institution, where its indispensable presence helps to soothe and cheer, or, by contrast, any place of entertainment where it enlivens the merrymakers; this adaptability of the piano perhaps tends to vulgarize it a little, yet it does not prevent its being a truly noble vehicle for the highest art of expression and interpretation in great masterpieces of music.

THE SPELL OF THE PIANO

The piano has also, I think, a humanizing and softening influence on the most unexpected people. I have found this so much amongst my travels, even hard business men, pioneers, backwoodsmen, rough miners from out West, farmers on the lonely prairies, sailors, sometimes the stokers from the ship's hold, people of all races and all colours can come under the spell of the piano.

It is told of Fouquet, the splendid and ill-fated minister of Louis XIV, that when speaking of music with one of the Court who was not an amateur, he exclaimed, "How, Monsieur, you care not for music, you do not play the clavecin, I am sorry for you, you are indeed condemning yourself to a dull old age!"

He was thinking no doubt of the joy which all can experience, even without being great performers, in picking out favourite tunes on the piano, stumbling over the themes of well-loved masterpieces and thereby reviving memories of enchanted hours passed in the concert hall or opera house.

We all know the unutterable satisfaction which even the most halting travesty of the real thing affords to the imagination of the devotee, and how much intensity and enthusiasm of expression make up for lack of execution!

What an inestimable boon, therefore, is the piano in the home! A friend, a companion, a comforter, a magician, all in one! Always ready to give its best, always sympathetic, unchanging, patient, without rancour for the outrages it sometimes has to suffer, at all times a never-failing resource.

No musical instrument has ever attained such universal popularity as the piano, because it is so easy to handle, so quick to give to those who ask from it. Therefore, almost everyone desires to have a piano in the home, and indeed something does seem strangely lacking if there is not one to be found anywhere throughout a house.

THE RIGHT CHOICE

If, therefore, the piano means so much to so many people, it surely follows that to know how to choose a good instrument at the outset is very important. Of course, pianos, like everything else, are largely judged and selected according to the degree of reputation enjoyed by their respective makers, and the person who has no special knowledge of what is a good or bad instrument is well advised to look for his piano at a first-class firm, who can show him examples by all the best producers. At any rate, he is safe to get a good article from them, and also find experts to advise him about the quality of the instrument. It is very unwise to go and buy a piano by any maker at an auction room unless it can be inspected by someone who possesses professional knowledge.

But it is not everything to have a first-class instrument; it is also of the utmost importance to look after it well. I cannot bear to go into a room and see a fine piano covered over with family photographs, and vases full of flowers, as one often does. The housemaid is sure to upset one of the vases, and the water trickling down through the hinges of the lid ruins the action; while the family portraits dance and jingle merrily as an accompaniment to the Beethoven Sonata or the exquisite Chopin study, and generally end by tumbling down with a bang, scratching all the polish off the top, and causing terrible trepidation to their owner, not to speak of the poor performer. I speak with feeling, from grim experience!

ITS WORST ENEMY

Most people know that a piano should not be kept in a draught, neither just under the window, nor between the door and the window. A long time of standing in such a position will spoil the best instrument, and if it is kept for many months in an unoccupied room it will deteriorate badly unless a fire is lit to dry the atmosphere from time to time. Damp is the worst enemy the piano can have. It is wise, too, if you wish to preserve your piano to the best advantage, to have it constantly tuned and examined by a first-class tuner. It is very much more difficult to repair satisfactorily a piano that has been systematically neglected (it can scarcely ever regain its original excellence) than to look after it carefully from the beginning, when it will last for years.

Size is an urgent point to be considered in the selection of a piano. An enormous and powerful Concert Grand is obviously unsuitable for a small and private drawing-room, and there is nothing better for a moderate-sized room than a Boudoir or Baby Grand. A good Upright is also by no means to be despised, for these are excellent instruments provided they have plenty of resonance, and are not too stiff in action.

MECHANICAL PLAYERS

One can scarcely discuss nowadays the merits of pianos in our homes without mentioning in connection with them the latest development of modern musical invention, the mechanical piano-players. Some musicians affect contempt for the mechanical piano-players and ridicule their value, but I do not agree with this view, for, though, no doubt, they cannot be said to contribute to the highest realms of musical expression, still I think they possess a very real value in that they educate the public taste, and enable people who would otherwise have no inclination or impulse to hear good music to become familiar with it. Therefore, let us not disparage the mechanical piano-players, even though they are trying neighbours in the next house when one is working or sleeping.

Of course, it is not quite the same thing, choosing a piano for one's private use, or selecting the Concert Grand from a professional point of view for a performance in a big hall. For instance, when I give a recital my piano is selected by me and my piano-maker some weeks before the concert from several special ones which I am in the habit of playing. It is tested as to its power of tone and resonance with reference to the acoustical properties of the hall. It is tuned, the action regulated, the pedals adjusted—in fact, it is prepared and brought into perfect condition, like a well-trained race-horse before it starts its race, so that it may be equal to all the demands imposed upon it.

If I were going to buy a piano for my own house, what should I look for? I should first of all search for one with a good even tone throughout, as well in the treble and bass registers as in the middle. Next, I should try the action by ascertaining if the keys repeat perfectly and whether the touch is easy and pliable under the fingers, and also whether the pedals act promptly.

But, as I have said before, it takes real knowledge to judge of such things oneself. If one has not had the opportunity of experience, the next best thing is to go to a first-class firm where only first-class instruments are kept and are looked after by experts.

And now, as a fitting finale, let me once more myself eulogize my beloved instrument and let me emphasize again what a wonderful work of human ingenuity it is. Who can but marvel when he hears the variety of its effects, the power and wealth of sound it possesses, its wonderful mechanical soul, the pedal, how it is able to produce such great emotions, tears, laughter, excitement, enthusiasm. It can give at the same time complete satisfaction to those of its unambitious devotees who seek only to pass away a few pleasant moments in evoking charming sounds and yet prove its stimulation as an instrument of superhuman difficulty and interest to those who desire to master it, and make it disclose all the richness and extent of its possibilities. And for such as are not easily tired or discouraged, the piano can be a glorious friend and companion, only they must have the will and perseverance, and above all talent and temperament, to inspire the instrument with life and master its secrets.

PART TWO

THE DAILY PIANIST

BEING EXTRACTS FROM FIVE-FINGER EXERCISES, SCALES,
ARPEGGI THIRDS, OCTAVES AS PRACTISED BY
MARK HAMBOURG

CHAPTER XV

FIVE-FINGER EXERCISES, SCALES AND ARPEGGIO EXERCISES

I STRONGLY advise the student, as he advances, to play through some of the Exercises every day, increasing the *Tempo* gradually but never playing them too rapidly, and paying careful attention to the articulation of the fingers. It is also advisable to play the scales and Arpeggio Exercises straight through without a break in each key.

All the Exercises given here should always be played by each hand separately.

The following Exercises can be played either *Forte* or *Piano*, and may be repeated three or four times, but without fatiguing the hand.

Each bar to be repeated four times.

The semibreves to be kept pressed down, and the crotchets to be played with the fingers marked under them, while counting aloud and lifting the different fingers about an inch from the keyboard.

1. Right hand.

The same exercise for the left hand to be played the same way.

2. Left hand.

SCALE AND ARPEGGIO EXERCISES

These scales should be practised every day with the accompanying arpeggio exercises in four different keys. Thus every scale and arpeggio in all the tonalities will be gone through twice during the week.

Thus : First day—C, D flat, D, E flat.
Second day—E, F, F sharp, G.
Third day—A flat, A, B flat, B.
Fourth day—Begin again on C, etc., etc.

Scales to be practised as below every day slowly with each hand separately, care being paid to the passage of the thumb and to the flexibility of the wrist.

Scales in C and Arpeggi.   Right hand.

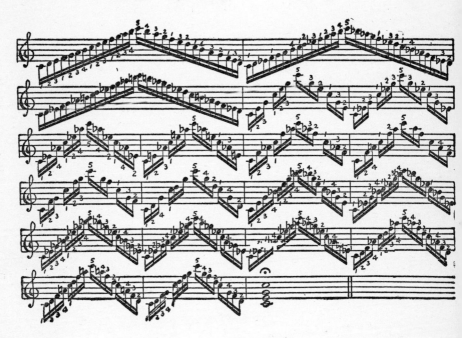

Scales in C and Arpeggi. Left hand.

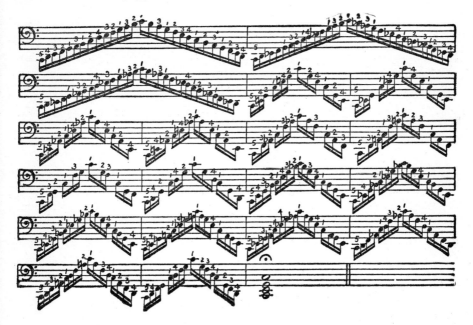

Scales in D flat and Arpeggi. Right hand.

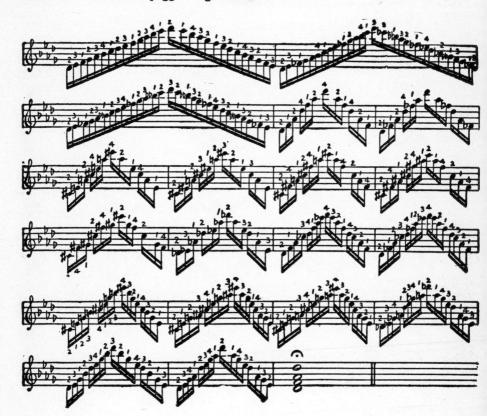

Scales in D flat and Arpeggi. Left hand.

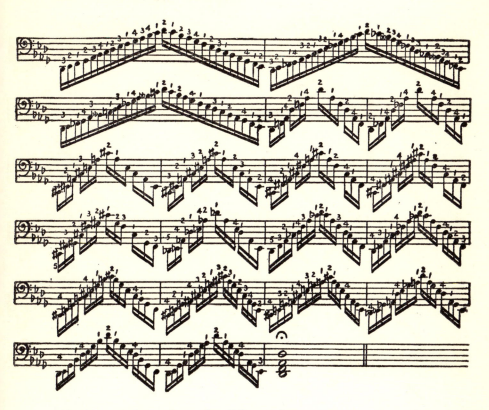

And so on throughout the different keys.

The fingering given in the C major example is similar in the keys of D, E, F, G, A, and B. For the E flat and B flat scales the fingering is the same as that given below.

Scales in B flat and Arpeggi. Right hand.

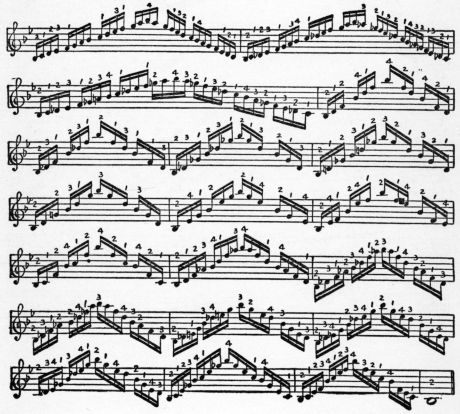

Scales in B flat and Arpeggi. Left hand.

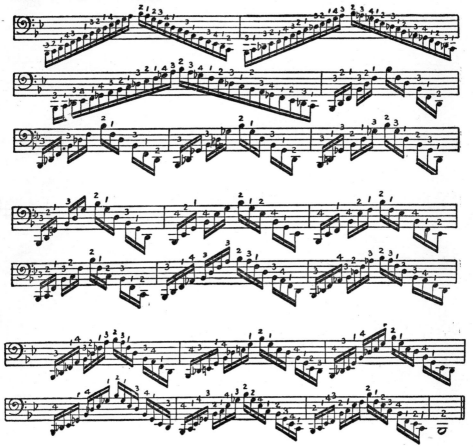

The fingering for the F sharp scale is as follows:

Scales in F sharp and Arpeggi. Right hand.

Scales in F sharp and Arpeggi. Left hand.

Chapter XVI

SCALES IN THIRDS AND OCTAVE EXERCISES

SCALES IN THIRDS WITH FINGERINGS MARKED

I. Right hand.

These fingerings can be used in all tonalities.

II. Left hand.

CHROMATIC THIRDS

III. Right hand. Minor thirds.

IV. Left hand. Minor thirds.

V. Right hand. Major thirds.

VI. Left hand. Major thirds.

OCTAVE EXERCISES

To be practised slowly and very staccato, wrist very loose.

I.

II.

OCTAVE JUMPS

I.

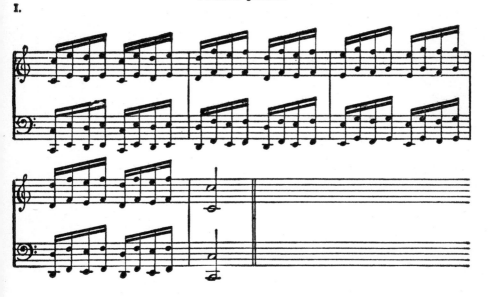

II.

REPEATING OCTAVES

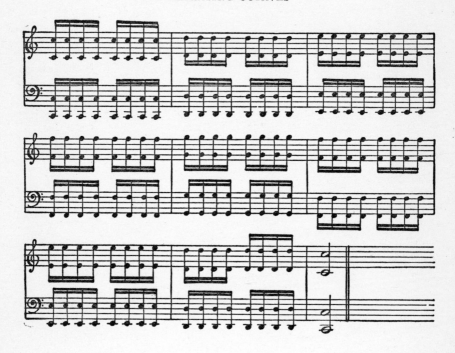

CHORD EXERCISES